AF379517

In Part

Writings by

Julie Ault

In Part

Writings by

Julie Ault

EDITED BY
Julie Ault and Nicolas Linnert

WITH AN INTRODUCTION BY
Lucy R. Lippard

Dancing Foxes Press and Galerie Buchholz

"A State of Unending Inquiry"

Lucy R. Lippard

Julie Ault has pioneered an elegant and provocative genre of art writing–as–art that strays from what is expected of art criticism (implying an adversarial relationship between artist and writer), which can only be good. I have often insisted that if anything an artist does is art then anything a writer does is writing. Ault complicates this notion because she *is* an artist, albeit an artist who has seldom produced an object or a solo show (her texts and exhibitions fill that role). Her curating, her art, her publications, and her activism are all of a piece. She could be called a socioconceptualist. Ault's work derives its depth and integrity from her conviction that research is "a state of unending inquiry." She will remain "involved with a subject matter for years or decades, manifesting findings in different forms and with shifting perspectives over time."

I've known Ault since 1980, through several different lives and across her geographically "nomadic existence." While her work continues to evolve and her reputation soars, she has stayed herself: smart, perceptive, disarmingly unpretentious, and politically savvy—though opposed to lefty polarization—and always inquiring. For seventeen years (1979–96), Group Material (she was a founding member) was Ault's school, her art, and her medium. Its collaborative process allowed the usually small cohort to ask the right questions: "What politics inform accepted understandings of art and culture? Whose interests are served by such cultural conventions? How is culture made, and for whom is it made?" She credits Group Material with cultivating ambiguity, always "trying to complicate definitions of both activism and art."

And these are the factors that have driven her for almost four decades. While other members (notably Tim Rollins and Doug Ashford) have also gone on to impressive collaborative projects and individual work, Ault has remained faithful, in her own way, to Group Material's original premise, building unique forms as she expands the possible functions and readings of art.

While examining the art "world" through the lens of lived experience and often brilliant analysis, Ault has tried to avoid conventional formats, and the understated emotional power of her work heightens its intellectual impact . . . or vice versa. Given my own chronic "escape attempts," I particularly admire Ault's invention of collaborative forms that allow her to stay on the margins of the art world while fully participating in its intellectual life. She continues to challenge hierarchies in the format of this book, using chronological excerpts to bypass conventional structures for critical anthologies. *In Part* is a kind of shorthand for her unorthodox trajectory. These simultaneously hermetic and accessible fragments can be intimate and tantalizing, reaching to the core of the writer's ideas and growth, while making the reader want more. It's a history of questioning, of *real* critical thinking, only distantly resembling much of the jargon-ridden academic brand.

The following fragments pay homage to this format, and to their author.

COLLABORATION

The late 1970s and early 1980s were a turbulent and energizing moment for activist artists, evoking the massive marches and outbursts of art we have been seeing since the 2016 election. The ascension of Ronald Reagan and his heartless trickle-down economics sparked innovations in demonstration art, street art, collaboration, and community alliances. We were up in (aesthetic) arms as a new generation (Ault's) joined the sixties generation (mine) in protests and projects. In New York, collaborations between individuals were paralleled by collectives with varying styles and objectives: Group Material, PAD/D, RePO History, Colab, ABC No Rio, Heresies, Fashion Moda, Art against Apartheid, WW3 Illustrated, Printed Matter, Franklin Furnace, the Alliance for Cultural Democracy, Cultural Correspondence, and Artists Call against US Intervention in Central America, and soon after, the Guerrilla Girls, Gran Fury, and the Women's Action Coalition (WAC), among others. Group Material's commitment to communication beyond the commercial art world paralleled the nascent "social practice" of feminist and community groups around the nation. The titles of Group Material's shows—*Americana, Democracy, Constitution*—betrayed the breadth of its concerns. In the twenty years since its demise, Ault has continued to work with others to address communal concerns, collaborating in various constellations with Martin Beck, Danh Vo, Roni Horn, Heinz Peter Knes, and James Benning, among others.

COLLECTING

Writing about Martin Wong's home, his "private cosmos," and the art that he acquired by sale or trade, Ault reflects on her own "collection"—"building blocks of identity"—uneasy about the term since her own considerable accumulation of art and objects has been an organic process. (Here too, I identify. If I ever write a "memoir," it will be a description of the objects in my home and the threads that bind them together and to my life.) An artist's accumulation always reflects friendships, influences, and idiosyncrasies. Photographs of Ault's home appeared in *Tell It to My Heart: Collected by Julie Ault*; they can be seen as private parallels to her public installations.

CONTEXT

"I work contextually, and a contextual approach means the material criteria and methodologies employed are contingent upon purpose, location, material parameters, and the issues at stake," wrote Ault in 2002. Eleven years later, she wondered, "Can contexts be, in effect, communicated?" That is indeed the challenging task of writers dealing with their own shared pasts in archives, historical accounts, and memoirs. Over decades, events tend to take on a rosier hue. (I think of the merciless "crit–self crit" sessions in feminist groups, which we can now laugh about.) We try to avoid romanticized nostalgia, to acknowledge failures, to re-create a pre-internet milieu that sounds medieval to today's youth. Context is rooted in place, as well as people and period. New York City in the eighties was more than one community, more than one place, with artists from "downtown," the Lower East Side (Loisaida), and the South Bronx working together. Ault's recent life in the relative solitude of the desert (Joshua Tree) and the forest (a cabin in Oregon), as well as her work and travels in Europe, have offered new contexts, which underlie projects like *Two Cabins* and other writings, such as those on artists Nancy Spero, David Wojnarowicz, and Roni Horn.

DECENTRALIZATION

Ever since the Art Workers' Coalition, "decentralization" has been the goal of many artists and groups who hope to revitalize the art world's margins and reach a broader audience. Each generation learns something from the last and comes a bit closer to the goal. Ault sees decentralization as an open-ended strategy privileging no single point of view; she "refuses to speak in terms of oppositions" in order not to "further replicate polarizing notions of culture." The trick to working within such a decentralized field, she writes, "is to find just enough mechanisms so that people can make relevant connections. This is precisely where art can be useful."

DILEMMAS

Since the 1940s, artists have struggled with their relationships to art institutions. Should they boycott museums to protest reactionary political positions and lack of support for artists? Should they actively, but oppositionally, participate when invited? Or should they just succumb in hopes of the power brought by success? Then there is the dilemma of voluntary (and involuntary) exclusion versus co-optation. Ault observes that most institutions have no artists on their boards (an issue first raised by the Art Workers' Coalition in 1969), invoking the powerlessness of individual artists to affect the mainstream: "It's inevitable that even if you are not intending to function in the marketplace, you are functioning in relation to that, and market and promotional principles determine the models of perception, despite how we view ourselves." Her critique extends, of course, to museums: "Were cultural institutions to regard their process as a creative one that is reflexive, doubt ridden, and productively discontinuous rather than a bureaucratic one that rigidly and arrogantly takes itself and its ways for granted, some benefits might ensue." Imagine a Museum of Modern Art or a Solomon R. Guggenheim Museum guided by the principles of Group Material.

EXHIBITION/INSTALLATION/PUBLICATION

"Exhibitions are key intersections where art and artifacts are made available to audiences, within which narratives, ideas, and sensations are activated." In accord with commitments to merging art and life, "high" and "low" culture, Group Material introduced mass-produced products into its installations as a way to encourage people to look at the blurred lines between aesthetic and commercial or quotidian choices and the "hierarchies of cultural economies." For example, Group Material's *People's Choice/ Arroz con Mango* (1981), mounted in its short-lived space on the Lower East Side, remains a personal favorite: members visited each apartment on their block asking for the residents' favorite objects, "art" or anything else. The results ranged from exhibited art to family pictures, political posters, sports trophies, needlework, and a snakeskin. Once it became clear that an exhibition could be a work of art in itself, the idea spread to museums, many of which have asked artists to reconceive the ways the museums' collections are presented. Ault still aims to "activate" neglected spaces and energies. She contends that, despite the burgeoning wave of curatorial studies, too little attention is paid to display strategies, observing that conventional museum display shows a "resistance to rethinking the terms of art after modernism." Since 2000, she has concentrated on publications, particularly the book form, as a means to broader circulation and longer lives for her ideas and those of the artists with whom she works.

HEROS

One of Ault's most unexpected (though not unreasonable) obsessions since 1995 has been with an artist she never met—the printmaker Sister Mary Corita (Kent), a nun for thirty years who worked with the Immaculate Heart Community in Los Angeles and advised her students to "consider everything an experiment." Corita made prints because they were a democratic form, and for years kept them out of the official aesthetic domain. Ault (who is partially responsible for Corita's international reputation) acknowledges that "Corita's exceptional qualities are potentially narrowed as her work is established in the art field. . . . [Her] crucial context is obscured." Ault's *Power Up* exhibition (a Corita title) created a joyful and unconventional context for both artwork and archival materials. In telling the tale of Corita's two archives, formal and informal, Ault is unabashedly enthusiastic: "I admire Corita the teacher, Corita the artist, Corita the catalyst, and mostly, Corita's ability to fuse celebration, aesthetics, and critical consciousness in her practice of life and art." (It's possible to attribute these same qualities to Ault herself.)

HISTORY

Because of my own current preoccupations, I am particularly intrigued by Ault's musings on memory, archives, and history. She recognizes "the violence of history writing" in its omissions, while suggesting that "historiography is a creative as well as an interpretive practice . . . it is a form of production." A vital archive must incorporate the "emotional intensity" that is too often weeded out in favor of order or propriety. Ault has also questioned the deceptively linear aspect of chronologies, while noting

Group Material's use of historical timelines. In her conversation with Marvin Taylor of the New York University Fales Library's Downtown Collection, he notes the risk that archival materials can die "the death of cataloguing, just like dried butterflies." Ault observes that there is no "complete story." "Physicists and philosophers widely agree that 'the flow of time' is a creation of consciousness that we rely on for order."

While looking back through the Group Material archives in the process of editing the book *Show and Tell: A Chronicle of Group Material*, Ault realized she had unwittingly told some "lies" (something that plagues me as well as I recall the past—I've found it's always best to be interviewed with peers so we can argue about and mutually recollect what actually went down). The task of *making history*, or "making past present (*a new tense?*)" sparked for Ault a series of hard questions, including "How does bringing documentation together imply shaping history and writing history? . . . What tense is the archive?" "How to make what is missing evident as a layer of historicizing?" And regarding the art world's addiction to novelty: "Can a culture rooted in actively forgetting its own history do anything other than repeat itself?" In the unique compendium that is *Show and Tell*, Ault does for Group Material what artist Greg Sholette has done for PAD/D and RePO History and Max Schumann has done for Colab. It is crucial that these important models remain in the public record, the public eye. They are all too relevant as we face an unprecedented need for intelligent and effective opposition in 2017.

PERSONAL

Friendship is a powerful impetus for much of Ault's work. This book includes moving eulogies to people who meant a great deal to her—her father (in an obituary in a Maine newspaper), her Aunt Jo, the vital Asian American curator Karin Higa, the artists Martin Wong and Felix Gonzalez-Torres. Group Material's 1989 *AIDS Timeline* was created when "nearly 18% of the US population [had] no medical insurance" (more shades of current issues . . .).

In Gonzalez-Torres's self-portrait, one of the recorded high-points is "Julie 1987," marking the date when they met. Time and its passing weave through this book. As he was dying of AIDS, Gonzalez-Torres sent a friend a clock with a note: "To more time." Ault suggests that his clock collection was "about facing time. Diagramming a situation of no escape."

In her fond account of (the still thriving) Tim Rollins, her early mentor and Group Material cofounder, bits of Ault's own autobiography emerge: the underachieving mall rat, the high school dropout with a kitchen-table-psychic mother, and the fifteen-year-old art student escaping small-town Maine who falls into a lifelong friendship with Rollins, the fearless gay activist, political artist-provocateur. Years later, we glimpse the college student in a leather jacket, already a known artist, who changed her political affiliation to Republican in order to infiltrate and understand conservativism ("Don't Be Yourself"). The Julie Ault we know today concluded that "mainstream politics were more cynical than anything I'd experienced [in ten years] in the cultural arena." Realizing that she was "unwilling to distort myself enough to fit in[to the electoral-politics establishment, even for interesting reasons]," she "went running back to art. . . . I matured." There are a few lovely, melancholy fragments about unnamed relationships: "It is good fortune to know the power *and* fragility of our connections to one another."

TODAY

In 1996, Ault wrote about "the collapse of the art market, the closing down of the public sphere by the political right, and the agenda to defund the National Endowment for the Arts." A decade later, she noted that "the income gap in 2000 was the widest it has been since 1979, and likely was the widest it has been in 70 years." Little did we know what was coming down the pike. In "The Double Edge of History"—one of seven essays published here in full, as markers of pivotal moments—Ault writes: "The United States did not suddenly become a conservative nation— it has always been one. One might conclude otherwise judging from a surface reading of the relatively liberal 'anything is possible' atmosphere in American culture. But its undercurrent—the origins, histories, and myths that shaped this country at its core—is deeply conservative." Elsewhere she ponders Liberace living in "palatial kitsch" within a world of mirrors: "Look at yourself in a mirror all your life," she warns, "and you'll see death at work."

All quotations from Ault are in this book.

Contents

Excerpts from writings, 1980–1997 1

The Double Edge of History 35

Excerpts from writings, 1997–2000 43

Widely Spaced at Eye Level 67

Excerpts from writings, 2000–2002 77

Archives in Practice 85

Excerpts from writings, 2002–2009 99

Tim 149

Excerpts from writings, 2009–2011 155

Don't Be Yourself 191

Excerpts from writings, 2012–2013 195

Active Recollection:
Archiving "Group Material" 207

Excerpts from writings, 2013–2014 221

Dishes, Diaries, and Cemeteries:
Josephine Fountain Tufts 233

Excerpts from writings, 2014–2018 237

Contributors 269
Acknowledgments 271

Group Material researches work from artists, nonartists, the media, the streets—from anyone interested in presenting socially critical information in a communicative and informal context. While our direct approach is oriented toward people not well acquainted with the specialized languages of fine art, we expect that our shows will be very refreshing for an audience that has a long-standing interest in questions of art theory and practice. In our exhibitions, Group Material reveals the multiplicity of meanings that surround any vital social issue so that people are introduced to a subject, making evaluations and further investigations on their own.

From Group Material, "Who, What, Where, When, Why, How." In *Inaugural Exhibition*. New York: Group Material, 1980. Exhibition handout.

Contrary to Kim Levin's assumptions ["The Whitney Laundry,"
Village Voice, April 9, 1985], Group Material wasn't used by the
Whitney to any greater extent than its resources and visibility
were used by us to present a critical model of what we believe an
American museum's biennial should be. . . . Does Levin really
believe it takes a clever critic to understand how institutions
manipulate the meaning and reception of culture? . . . If you
really want a "radical shakeup," why stop at the Biennial? The
entire culture industry needs to be overhauled. *Americana* is but
one small demonstration toward a program of cultural change.
It was not designed for the Whitney, or for art critics, but for the
large public, which Levin contemptuously reduces to "students,
tourists, novices, and art investors."

From Group Material (Tim Rollins, Mundy McLaughlin, Julie Ault, Doug Ashford),
"Letter to the *Village Voice.*" *Village Voice,* April 16, 1985.

Contradiction—between ideals and lived reality, between wealth
and poverty, between dominant culture and ethnic difference—is
the fundamental historical tradition of our United States. Group
Material's *Constitution* is a critical tribute to this national condition
—this primal American desire for individual freedom that at
once vindicates and threatens the premises of our most revered
historic document. A constitution is also a walk. Walking through
our exhibition, you are walking through the principles of the
Constitution made visible. You add to this exhibition with
the lived experience and actions of your daily lives, transforming
Constitution from a noun to a verb, into social action.

From Group Material (Tim Rollins, Julie Ault, Doug Ashford), *Constitution*, p. 6.
Philadelphia: Temple University, 1987. Exhibition catalogue.

Julie Ault: Some people think of power in black or white terms—no matter what you do in a museum is negated by the fact that it's in a museum, you've sold out. We obviously disagree.

In many exhibitions we have included "outsider" art, work by people with no formal art training, and also practitioners whose work may not even be called art. Randall Morris, codirector of the Cavin-Morris Gallery, which represents outsider artists, commented once that if you look at art making from a global perspective, the word *mainstream* is meaningless. Take that word away and *others* would be outside of nothing. . . . There is no outside or inside. Ultimately, that's what we're working toward: a redefinition and reclaiming of culture.

Felix Gonzalez-Torres: That's what happens in our shows. Hierarchy is broken down. You can see a piece by Haim Steinbach next to a piece by Bessie Harvey, an untrained artist from South Carolina. But when people write about the exhibitions, they mention only the familiar names and for the most part overlook people who might not be in prominent galleries.

Doug Ashford: Our exhibitions are a kind of analysis where artworks decipher, comment, enlighten, legitimize each other. Often the social purpose of a particular artwork has been clouded by the way it gets seen within the market and the museum. The concept of a show and the juxtaposition with other practices, some not even by artists, show that art has other possible functions and readings.

From Group Material (Doug Ashford, Julie Ault, Felix Gonzalez-Torres), "Dialectical Group Materialism," interview by Jim Drobnick. *Parachute* 56 (October/November/December 1989): p. 31.

In response to grassroots activism, the Food and Drug Administration (FDA) approves aerosol Pentamidine for prevention of AIDS-related pneumonia (PCP). This is the first time a drug has been approved because of community-based research. Pentamidine increased in cost from $25 in 1984 to $200 in 1989, per dose/per month.

The opening session of the Fifth International AIDS Conference in Montreal is taken over by PWAs and AIDS activists calling for more inclusion of people with AIDS in research. ACT UP releases "A National AIDS Treatment Research Agenda," which outlines principles for conducting clinical trials: involving PWAs in trial design, emphasizing drugs for opportunistic infections, creating more flexible protocols, broadening entry requirements, avoiding use of placebos, and establishing criteria other than death rate for judging whether drugs are effective.

A study sponsored by the insurance industry shows that 37 million people, nearly 18% of the US population, have no medical insurance.

26% of adolescents who were diagnosed with AIDS in 1989 contracted HIV through heterosexual intercourse. AIDS cases among 15-year-olds in New York City increased 40% between 1987 and 1989.

David Duke, former leader of the Knights of the Ku Klux Klan, is elected to the Louisiana State Legislature on the Republican ticket.

From Group Material (Karen Ramspacher, Felix Gonzalez-Torres, Julie Ault, Doug Ashford), *AIDS Timeline.* Matrix Gallery, University Art Museum, University of California, Berkeley, 1989. Exhibition wall text and handout.

Julie Ault: Originally we thought, oh, Berkeley, California, we're doing a show about AIDS in San Francisco.

Felix Gonzalez-Torres: Little did we know.

JA: Then we came out and we were naive; we realized that Berkeley and San Francisco are like worlds apart in many ways. . . .
  We looked at some statistical studies that had been done about people's—university students'—understanding of transmission of AIDS and if they were practicing safe sex or not, and then the ultimate thing was what we had for the democracy wall outside . . .
  Larry [Rinder] had someone make a tape with a series of questions that were asked of people on the street, which in this case, outside of the museum, were students walking by. Our first question was: "How does AIDS affect you and your lifestyle?" Thirty-one students were interviewed and every one of them said, "It doesn't affect me at all" or "It doesn't affect me much because I don't really sleep around," which was the final quote that we used for outside of the building. And then we became very much aware that okay, AIDS—there are no givens here—it's not like people are going to know any of this history and we really have to start from scratch and build on that.

Doug Ashford: That people's unawareness is part of the policy, you know, and I think the democracy wall does that very well right now. It starts off with whoever responded to the tape by saying, "AIDS doesn't affect me because I don't sleep around," and then it ends with former surgeon general Koop saying, "You know it, I know it, we all know it: the government hasn't done anything." And that these two statements are the flip side of the same thing.

From Group Material (Felix Gonzalez-Torres, Karen Ramspacher, Doug Ashford, Julie Ault), interview by Maria F. Porges. *Shift* 4, no. 1 (1990): p. 23.

The subject that no one in the art world wants to talk about is usually politics. Yet, because every social or cultural relationship is a political one, we regard an understanding of the link between politics and culture as essential. "Politics" cannot be restricted to those arenas stipulated as such by professional politicians. Indeed, it is fundamental to our methodology to question every aspect of our cultural situation from a political point of view, to ask, "What politics inform accepted understandings of art and culture? Whose interests are served by such cultural conventions? How is culture made, and for whom is it made?"

From Group Material (Julie Ault, Doug Ashford, Felix Gonzalez-Torres), "On Democracy." In *Democracy | A Project by Group Material.* Ed. Group Material and Brian Wallis. Discussions in Contemporary Culture, no. 5, p. 1. Seattle: Bay Press; New York: Dia Art Foundation, 1990.

Julie Ault: I don't think that *beauty* is a bad word, but because beauty is so subjective, it's a sticky word to use. The idea of accessibility and making it inviting can mean obviously it's not just for the audience either, it's for ourselves. The aesthetic decisions we make are determined by the world as we see it and our culture. It's not like we would throw those away and say, let's only do red and black 'cause that's political . . . It doesn't make sense. I think, because our aesthetics have a lot to do with popular culture and media, this is the way of communicating now. A lot of it has to do with competing to attract people's attention to the issues and ideas that we're working with. We're interested in something much more popular than traditionally what would be defined as leftist.

Doug Ashford: But then that gets tricky too because although we're trying ideally to popularize something, at the same time we're interested in questioning what people would consider popular. Why do things become popular? There are private forces influencing what people like. Corporate culture sometimes determines all of this for us. Remember New Coke? Those of us who resist the dominant culture should see ideological systems as self-generating. Institutions can create desire almost overnight. When New Coke came out there was a political movement to bring back Old Coke. It was a grassroots thing. What we got was Classic.

JA: I think that a lot of people just don't see aesthetics or method or the way things work as being anywhere equal to the subject. The problem, say, with "political art" is that it's political art. It's not art that's political. The politics are 90 percent and then there's 10 percent, which is just how to do it, how to get it out there. Whereas we really see this marriage of form and content as being crucial to the politics and to communicating political ideas.

From Group Material (Doug Ashford, Julie Ault), interview by Elizabeth A. Brown. In *Social Studies: 4 + 4 Young Americans*. Ed. William J. Chiego and Larry J. Feinberg, pp. 46–47. Oberlin: Allen Memorial Art Museum, Oberlin College, 1990. Exhibition catalogue.

The Rhetorical Image Resource Room was intended to disrupt the passive role offered to visitors in most museums, to actively engage participants in a critical and analytical process, and to foreground the value of viewers' experiences in art interpretation. It aimed to demonstrate that meaning is not a preexisting entity lurking below the surface, which only the scholar can uncover using the special tools of expertise, but is something that is socially constructed, fragmentary, and contingent on the position of the "knower." Our goal was to subtly shift the discursive focus onto voices, which are seldom if ever heard, to blur the distinction between speaker and listener, and to problematize the separation between authoritative and nonauthoritative positions within the museum.

From Julie Ault and Susan Cahan, *Rhetorical Image Resource Room: A Viewer Participation Project*, pp. 7–8. New York: New Museum of Contemporary Art, 1991. Exhibition brochure.

The image of the word *FREEDOM* printed on a wallet was our entry into this subject and consequent project. This wallet, purchased in a variety store about ten years ago, was strikingly overt, more like a work of art than a mass-produced product. Such a visually concrete conflation of democracy and capitalism articulates the common public confusion between these two ideas, these two merged systems. The freedom wallet is suggestive of conflicting interior and collective experiences—frustration, rage, hope, anxiety, fear, desire, disappointment, and yearning.

Ambivalences we experience engendered by dissolution and reformulation of a generalized social sphere must be distinguished from political ambivalence. What appears now to be a market of possibilities, expansive enough to serve every need, desire, and specificity, is, with closer scrutiny, a reformulation that seductively announces its responsive character, while ultimately upholding social divisions along traditional and familiar lines of inequity. This inherently biased "free-market" social system does not acknowledge itself as ideologically unified in service of (its own) social order, rendering it all the more effective.

From Group Material (Julie Ault, Thomas Eggerer, Jochen Klein, Doug Ashford), *Market*, n.p. Munich: Kunstverein München, 1995. Exhibition catalogue.

One morning he walked into a room and removed all his
clothes—jeans, T-shirt, belt, socks, underwear, and shoes—
leaving them behind in a pile on the floor: *What's Left* (1992).
The fragile intimacy of what was casually left, like a child's room
kept intact by his parents long after his departure, conveys
and contains the missed person—his last touch, his aroma and
warmth. And what did it mean for him to leave, to disappear?

Our universe appears remarkably stable, but scientists say it's
changing with greater velocity than human perception can register. I wonder what the space is like between the sun and the
moon during an eclipse and if it bears any resemblance to
the space of two people's memories of their time together.

From *Beyond, behind, within*. Ed. Jim Hodges, p. 18. Annandale-on-Hudson, NY:
Center for Curatorial Studies, Bard College; New York: CRG Gallery, 1995.
Artist's book.

It's fascinating how people arrange their belongings—books, art, all sorts of stuff.

Thought processes (chaotic, ambivalent, controlled) are indicated, at least superficially.

One gets a sense of another's composition, boundaries, and permeability. Lucy's coffee table is always piled high to overflowing with a wildly diverse mixture of books and journals, an unarranged assembly—informed by mistrust of hierarchy and suspicion of order and fixed systems. There's always room for more in this environment, which, like her work, continues to grow in volume and variety.

I once heard Lucy described as a "national treasure" and always liked that portrayal. What should be collectively treasured? What should be held and revered over time? Integrity of process . . . dialogue . . . the simplicity of treating each other well . . . flexibility? Operational democracy seems so out of reach these days; maybe it always was, but somehow it's still a dear ideal and practice. Dispensing with intellectual and emotional borders that require dogmatic defense is a lifelong process, one that Lucy chooses to make transparent and public through her writing. Her willful and reasoned resistance to categories, borders, labels, compartments, and containment is central to cultural democracy.

Moving target as national treasure.

From "The Absence of Borders." In *Sniper's Nest: Art That Has Lived with Lucy R. Lippard*. Ed. David Frankel, p. 3. Annandale-on-Hudson, NY: Center for Curatorial Studies, Bard College, 1996. Exhibition catalogue.

Martin Beck and Mathias Poledna: In the invitation, poster, and brochure image you use to publicize your exhibition *Cultural Economies*, the terms *growth* and *decay* mark a motif that also seems to comment on the subject of the project, the history of alternative art practices in New York.

Julie Ault: The collapse of the art market, the closing down of the public sphere by the political right, and the agenda to defund the National Endowment for the Arts have all coincided in a way that alternative spaces and the nonprofit art world are in a state of decline. This pressure is partly external but maybe even more so internal as it is also a result of the alternative-space idea having been institutionalized and having become structural for the art-world system. My intention is to look at and trace the impact that alternative initiatives have had in themselves but also their effect on the cultural mainstream, such as museum culture. I also want to reflect the reasons for this decline in relation to how alternative spaces function and what their policies are. The perception of alternative spaces being the children of the commercial galleries is in fact true, but that's not what their origins were.

Throughout the eighties, this arena offered possibilities for developing new social formations to work within. But over the last few years one senses a burnout that I see being directly connected to extreme privatization. In the Reagan era, the social privatization of all spheres has crept up on all of us, but the effects of Reagan-Bush politics are felt much stronger now than they were at the beginning of the eighties.

From "Opposition as Alternative Container," interview by Martin Beck and Mathias Poledna. *Springerin* 2, no. 1 (March–April 1996): p. 25. Published in German.

The more voices speaking about a time, an event, a feeling, the richer and fuller history becomes, perhaps only to break totally, as a contained image or narrative, from the density and scope of contradictory descriptions. There can be no complete story, no real story, no decisive reading of events or their meanings. The more points of view there are, the more discussion there is, the more unmanageable the story becomes. And the more inspiring.

From "Why Is Today the Same as Every Other Day?" In *Cultural Economies: Histories from the Alternative Arts Movement, NYC*. Ed. Julie Ault, p. 8. New York: Drawing Center and Real Life Magazine, 1996. Exhibition catalogue.

The dedication page that prefaces Toni Morrison's stunning novel *Sula* reads: "It is sheer good fortune to miss somebody long before they leave you. This book is for Ford and Slade, whom I miss although they have not left me." The sentiment that these words evoke struck me as remarkably mature. I imagined Morrison's view was rooted in emotional liberation, arrived at via a uniquely shaped configuration of pain and accumulated losses. Her words also sparked an internal disturbance. It's a fine line, treating someone as though they're there, which they are, while simultaneously glimpsing potential and probable futures—holding two (or more) tenses in mind.

I tried to appropriate Morrison's maturity as well as the good fortune and gave him a copy of her book. He was sick at the time, the dreaded fate coming closer. I wanted him to read the dedication as though it were me saying those words to him. The good fortune lies in not taking someone's presence for granted. It is good fortune to know the power *and* fragility of our connections to one another.

From "Everything Is More Complicated Than Visible." In *Present Tense: Nine Artists in the Nineties*, p. 10. San Francisco: San Francisco Museum of Modern Art, 1997. Exhibition catalogue.

Pauline Boudry: Group Material had started to work in 1980 after a decade where a lot of activism and political discourses had developed. These groups often had had to defend their specific positions separately. For Group Material, was it a consequent evolution that these issues should be taken over together?

Julie Ault: Personally I am not interested in expediently separating out issues that I don't think can be separated. In Group Material, too. We never sat down and articulated, "We have to make a show where every possible link is made," but that is the way we have worked because that is the way culture works, interconnected. It does not really make sense to make those distinctions, to make a show about sexism without linking it to the whole network of power relations and social dynamics. I do not want to keep repeating the list, racism, class, homophobia etc., you know, the enemies or whatever. But it has never made sense as general practice to separate those out, because that is not the way it works. They exist together as a network of power. Sexism depends on homophobia is linked to racism depends on economic stratification, etc. It is necessary to represent those links and the whole and not fall in the trap of thinking that they can be treated independently or autonomously. This does not foreclose the fact that there are situations and contexts when one kind of violence or discrimination is particularly operable or emphasized, or where a single issue or topic should be privileged for a particular aim.

PB: At the same time as the exhibitions reflect many points of views, as not to reproduce systems of exclusions and authoritative discourse on an issue, the projects of Group Material are signed by a collective name. What are the limits of this collective signature?

JA: I think Group Material has tried to counter signature identification and inherent limitations in that by trying to find as many ways as possible to avoid being pigeonholed, sequestered, or identified as one thing. We have worked with different forms: interior exhibitions, publications, making projects in advertising space, sometimes as producers, sometimes as contractors, sometimes as organizers, and so on. I will not say we failed, but it's inevitable that even if you are not intending to function in the marketplace, you are functioning in relation to that, and market and promotional principles determine the models of perception, despite how we view ourselves. Group Material became by repetition of forms and interests identified in a certain way. Also, we do have a style, or a vocabulary of style. And I am aware that at some point in our history our forms became formulas. We have not made commodities or functioned commercially but are identified both as an institution and, in a sense, as an artist. A handle or sign(ature) is required in order to gain the "authority" to utilize certain platforms—even if you want to use them to redescribe authority.

From interview by Pauline Boudry. In *Environ 27 ans (peut-être un peu plus . . .)*. Ed. Martine Anderfuhren, Pauline Boudry, and Anne-Julie Raccoursier, pp. 49–50. Geneva: Société des Arts de Genève Classe des Beaux-Arts, 1997. Exhibition catalogue.

If the criticism of the 42nd Street project [organized by Creative
Time, 1993] *is founded on an analysis of what was there before,
there is obviously some constructive critique of the changes in this
zone, of its "Disneyfication." But is there not some nostalgia for what
was there, the sex industry? Why was this more real in respect to the
family-oriented culture being promoted now?*

Julie Ault: It's less nostalgia and more anger at the way the private initiative with the proper power base is able to totally demolish a community in the name of so-called public good and using the vocabulary of public morality for a private commercial agenda. Times Square has been changed without any thought or solutions for the people that operated commercially and inhabited it formerly, who have now been displaced. The City of New York—the same one that doesn't have the funds to build adequate housing for low-income people or adequately house its homeless population—found $35 million to acquire the last private buildings on 42nd Street ($180 million had been spent between 1990 and 1993 to buy others). It's not a matter of whether I liked it how it was before and don't now, I can get touristic and voyeuristic pleasure from either, but it's the political process that's informed by economics and the selective privatization process I want to emphasize and not the result of getting rid of the sex industry in Times Square.

From Q&A to the lecture "Generazione delle Immagini III: Public Art," City Council for Youth and Sport, Milan, 1997. In *La Città Degli Interventi—The City of Interventions*. Ed. Roberto Pinto, pp. 105–6. Milan: Commune di Milano, 1997.

The Double Edge of History

The United States did not suddenly become a conservative nation—it has always been one. One might conclude otherwise judging from a surface reading of the relatively liberal "anything is possible" atmosphere in American culture. But its undercurrent—the origins, histories, and myths that shaped this country at its core—is deeply conservative.

Culture is one arena where the paradoxical condition of American society frequently manifests. For example, just as national and state arts endowments finally revised their policies to ensure nondiscriminatory consideration and support in the field, calls for the termination of government arts subsidies grew louder and more persistent. In response to accusations of elitism and bigotry, many institutions have aimed to be more inclusive in recent decades. Yet just as many mainstream establishments sought to reform exclusionary practices and to "reach out to new audiences," the threatened demise of the already crippled National Endowment for the Arts (NEA) effectively erodes art's potential social functions, simultaneously sending museum directors on the hunt for financing through corporate partnerships and chasing after marketing consultants for money-making strategies.

The salient terms deployed in public discourse on cultural funding and other civic issues have been predominantly defined in support of conservative and commercialist agendas. Social agency, American-style, is linked to survival and accomplishment in marketplaces and in promotional culture at large. Consider, for instance, that the highly inflated art market of the 1980s was followed—not coincidentally—in 1989 by attacks on public cultural funding from the fundamentalist religious right with subsequent attacks from like-minded members of Congress. Glossy magazine coverage glamorizing the art world and reports of record-breaking prices for contemporary art made ideal pre-conditions for congressional initiatives to "get the government out of culture," leaving artists to fend for themselves economically and philosophically.

During the 1970s and early 1980s, often with help from the NEA, many alternative spaces and group structures were established as constructive responses to the explicit and implied limitations in the commerce-oriented art world. Critical efforts to theorize representation as a contested arena and to create venues for self-representation were generated and accommodated in these sites. One such entity was the artists' collaborative Group Material, which in the fall of 1996 articulated its ending.

Particular cultural circumstances produce particular responses and activities. Group Material cohered around shared desires to fuse political interests and art in practice, and to articulate collaboration as a socially engaged practice. When the group formed in 1979 in New York City, we were friends and friends of friends. The goals were to make a work space for ourselves and to have fun. We sought, in our formation and projects, to counter the competitive art system as well as a host of interlocking discriminations and elitisms evident in how art was then being taught, displayed, described, and distributed. Perhaps Group Material's most significant act of activism was to begin itself.

Within the first couple of years, decisions were made to protect the group from a potential path of unnecessary perpetuation. We considered the common trajectory of numerous alternative organizations that had rapidly institutionalized themselves and reasoned that if we refused those processes and rejected their trappings—a stable location, salaried positions, standardized procedures and programming—continuity would be based on desires and needs of the group's participants, along with a perceived complementary imperative in the art field. The group itself was our medium, and flexibility was crucial—so that it could expand or shrink, redirect focus, and change direction at will.[1]

Group Material's activities were most concentrated throughout the 1980s, years of relatively generous public funding for the arts, clear presidential enemies, and an active do-it-yourself atmosphere, which permeated cultural production in multiple fields and disciplines.

Group Material was primarily concerned with making situations within art and cultural contexts that focused on topical issues and political and social circumstances—no lasting objects, no permanence intended. In order to avoid marginalization and be effectual in presenting models of how we thought cultural description and politicized questioning might be practiced, we frequently utilized mainstream venues such as museums and advertising spaces. The group's viability as an independent entity working temporally within such existing establishments was dependent on an institutional "need" for "respectful" contestation—for something like Group Material (collaborative, political, pluralist, stylish, etc.)—and on our ability to negotiate various social relations, agencies, and situations with the right proportions of fixed and unfixed identity and signature.

From 1986 on, we intermittently reflected on whether we still found our process fulfilling and how our work was being received. We discussed whether to disband or keep going and repeatedly chose to reinvest. But over time a shift in self-perception occurred—in combination with members' growing financial

---

[1] For the first year or so, Group Material consisted of thirteen members: Hannah Alderfer, George Ault, Julie Ault, Patrick Brennan, Liliana Dones, Yolanda Hawkins, Beth Jaker, Mundy McLaughlin, Marybeth Nelson, Marek Pakulski, Tim Rollins, Peter Szypula, Michael Udvardy. But by the summer of 1981, we had shrunk to three—Mundy, Tim, and myself. Doug Ashford joined in 1982. In 1986 Mundy left, and in 1987 Felix Gonzalez-Torres came into the group. Also in 1987, Tim left. In 1989, Karen Ramspacher joined and remained through 1991. Felix stopped participating actively in 1991. And late in 1994, Thomas Eggerer and Jochen Klein joined, remaining through 1996.

needs and desires to work individually and in other collaborative constellations—that made for a series of turning points within the group's internal dynamics and public functioning.

At some unpinpointable time, what had been a productive and generative foundation (a history) transformed into webs of expectations, both internal to the group and from outside sources. At some unpinpointable time, the forms we developed and utilized (salon-style designed thematic exhibitions, democracy walls, roundtable discussions, advertising space as exhibition site) became overly familiar—if not to audiences, then to ourselves. An influence in the process of enforced continuity is the cultural treadmill we boarded in hopes of utilizing every opportunity and venue as a platform. This movement into acute self-consciousness—of GM as "an artist" (first name Group, last name Material), objectified, and "in history"—marked a threshold crossed. From enthusiasm to being jaded is not a simple procedure. The group rhythm we had relished had been disrupted.

Along with our awareness—through experience, not conjecture—of the situations described above came another realization. By 1992 it was apparent that our desires to symbolically and concretely break down hierarchies and diffuse borders between "high" and "low," public and private, producer and consumer, etc., were being visibly addressed by many mainstream cultural institutions. It remains unclear to what extent such efforts that appear to redress previous systemic biases are responding to pressures, are strategically seductive, and how deeply institutions are and will be effected over time.

Questions emerged at this juncture. If we took a break, could we digest the differences a decade made and reinvent our practice so it would be fulfilling for us as well as filling a need in culture? What would disbanding mean in respect to the evaluation of the group and in respect to our professional identities? Would it be irresponsible to sacrifice the cachet the group had achieved? If we chose to continue, could new members be integrated in a productive fashion?

From 1993 to 1996, Group Material worked on only one project each year. Diminishing the volume of projects had positive effects and afforded us time to consider options for the group's continuance or dispersal, but it was also becoming clear that Group Material's history was a presence, which in various ways overdetermined our then present as well as our imagined future.

In 1996, seventeen years after it originated, Group Material formally self-dissolved. When asked why it ended, I hear another question—more latent—"What is the tragedy of Group Material?" It's sort of like being asked to perform one's own autopsy. Because of an accumulation of histories and reasons that cannot adequately or accurately be communicated, its active life finished. There is no agreed-upon narrative—tragic or triumphant—but rather a mix of accomplishments, thoughts, regrets, relief, desires, recollections, and questions.

Group Material's dissolution does not negate its history, history that at least for now remains largely unhistoricized. Should this history be documented in a book that could last and circulate? If so, by whom—its former members or an art historian? The fragments that contribute to any history can be selected and configured to make a particular structure—to shape the past and/or to mobilize the present. That Group Material has an interest in its own historicization, in how it's done, is intrinsic to the group's working paradigm. Producing such a book is enticing "as a project" in which the investigative and representational methods Group Material utilized would be mirrored and enacted in relation to its own history. Conversely there is a certain appeal in preserving the ephemeral aspect of the entire project by not bringing documentation together in one packaged history. Ambivalence about any such enterprise perseveres.

The hierarchies of cultural economies are reproduced in respect to what "becomes" part of history. With no associated objects or projects currently circulating in the art economy, efforts disappear—they are written out of its history. Conferring value in this way is a strategy to marginalize certain positions and enterprises. The histories of groups and collectives often remain unwritten—no money (it takes money to write history), no marquee appeal. Another contributing factor is a feature of group structure itself. As discursive and multivoiced, it is inherently complicated and treacherous to represent.

There are certain challenges specific to a process of the historicization of the conditions and impacts of group activities. For a complex understanding of activities that sought to divert and subvert master narratives, it's important to propose alternatives to streamlined narratives that operate along linear logic in which one thing leads to another. Providing an orderly view or encapsulation of debated events and meanings is to some extent a revision of events whereby conflicts and contradictions are ultimately resolved, at least in their representation.

The dangers of taking pleasure in the past and the benefits of remembering in order to reinvent are not clearly posted. There is the risk of peddling nostalgia, of getting lost and/or paralyzed in emotionally inflected territory in which re-creation of the past obscures and replaces (or displaces) the present. To aid critical understanding of past specificities, and their effect in the present, it seems more productive to consider loose continuums of production than to provide a form of periodization as punctuation.

How to balance multiple relations to history? Alternatives to traditional historiographic practices might trace spatial and temporal configurations of interconnected events, activities, and associations of ideas nested in cultural circumstances, and by design provide spaces for multiple meanings, conflicting imaginations, conflicting "facts," and partiality. Historiography might be approached akin to artistic methodologies, utilize juxtaposition and artistic license, render ambivalently rather than declaratively, and ultimately acknowledge, not only in principle but as part of a historicizing method itself, that historiography is a creative as well as an interpretive practice: that it is a form of production.

The list of group entities, alternative spaces, and organizations that have dissolved or closed their doors seems to signal distress and dysfunction for certain critical strategies, as well as the disintegration of nonprofit networks. Although some organizations that wanted to were unable to survive, many that are now gone were strategic and time-based by purpose (i.e., protest strategies are usually one step in processes advocating social change). Other endeavors have become institutionalized, incorporated into larger entities, reconfigured, and so on. But facts always have multiple meanings. For a less bleak panorama, one should register the fact that critical alternative activities have altered accepted notions of possible functions and definitions of art.

Perhaps the most pressing question in respect to dissolutions of Group Material and other groups is, Should they be read as a barometer or as emblematic of the so-called dismal state of art-field activism? In my opinion, claims that collective production's "time" has passed or that certain strategies are no longer relevant are absurd. One cannot in good faith cite the endings of Gran Fury, Women's Action Coalition (WAC), Group Material, or any other collective entity as evidence of such claims. Perhaps for some who do, it's a wish. Perhaps for others, it is an alibi. Uncertainty over the status and future of oppositional processes and structures continues, but it is counterproductive to translate that uncertainty into pessimism.

Springerin 3, no. 3 (Fall 1997): pp. 57–59. Published in German.

Julie Ault: Many of your exhibitions utilize a decentralization model, projects feeding into or coexisting alongside one another nonhierarchically. Within such a decentralized field, how do you expect people to navigate through all the material? Imposing a heavy-handed institutional voice as the viewer's guide through the show is just as problematic as delivering massive amounts of material without facilitating interconnections of meaning. The trick is to find just enough mechanisms so that people can make relevant connections. This is precisely where art can be useful, in emphasizing the salient points within a theme or subject. Could you talk about your aesthetic allegiances?

Renate Lorenz: Aesthetics always marks and creates a relation—to other aesthetics used in artworks historically, as well as those in advertising and in products springing from political movements. If an exhibition is aesthetically diverse, you can get an idea of this field of relations. I'm not talking about diversity made on purpose but diversity that emerges from the different backgrounds of the participants. Moreover, aesthetics should be understood as a field of regulation in terms of who and what is represented, what kind of knowledge is presumed and produced.

Sylvia Kafehsy: I like to go to exhibitions where there are storyboards or something similar—something very attractive that pulls you in. Our shows were really too big. I found that if you have too much documentation, the show resembles a bookstore. But sometimes it's not very important what a show looks like. It's more about how you work and how you involve other people.

Marion von Osten: *Sex & Space* (1996) was primarily a process-oriented show, which brought with it a complex set of reflections from people in various fields—architecture, politics, sociology. But the show also generated problems in terms of engaging a broader public. For example, the lectures by the invited participants structured the show overall, but the production-space

studio atmosphere made it difficult for the so-called public to
get involved. A publication will take the discussion back to the
public, but I would have liked to solve this problem within
the exhibition itself. The use of the space in relation to the issue
of the public was not adequately planned. In the future, I would
propose that visualization stay in the center of our interests.

From "Shedhalle '94–'96," interview with Renate Lorenz, Sylvia Kafehsy, Ursula
Biemann, and Marion von Osten. *Documents*, no. 10 (Fall 1997): pp. 48–49.

In *Power Up* specific context is constructed. The intended effect is that upon entering the exhibition the viewer crosses a threshold into a dynamic visual and contextual environment. Ephemeral materials relating to how, when, and why the artworks were produced are an important part of *Power Up*. Context implies symbiotic processes between images and ideas. It challenges any clear-cut notion of separation between objects, exhibitions, and the outside world. Context is the active ground on which circumstances, features, and relations—between people, events, ideas, activities, and objects—are not fixed but are constantly in dialogue.

The primary juxtaposition in *Power Up* is of these two artists who are not readily united either historically or formally. In the exhibition design, the artworks are newly situated in actual and potential relations. Such juxtapositions and spatial arrangements render the works interactive in multiple combinations. Works commingle in circumstances that open up new and unprecedented relations and meanings.

From *Power Up: Reassembled Speech, Interlocking Sister Corita and Donald Moffett*, pp. 5–6. Hartford, CT: Wadsworth Atheneum, 1997. Exhibition brochure.

Many rules of legibility central to the formalism of modernist design principles are broken in Corita's work. In her hands, language is excerpted, disassembled, reassembled, and recontextualized. Typography is distorted, faced backward, and turned upside down. Letter forms are ungrounded, float, and interlock. To decipher her editorial vision and syntax, the viewer must become mentally acrobatic. These destabilizing techniques mirror Corita's own changing relationship with church officialdom and its hierarchies in the most personal realms of her life.

Although authority is conferred on certain kinds of speech that are readily preserved in public records and historical archives, vernacular speech such as ad phraseology arrives and disappears from circulation swiftly. Corita's work does not reproduce the hierarchies common to such categorizing systems of information. In any given print, as well as across her production, voices—both respected and denigrated, both commercial and philosophical—are brought into proximity when forming non-linear narratives. In Corita's art, the fugitive elements of ephemeral culture are given permanence.

From "Somebody Had to Break the Rules." *Springerin* 3, no. 4 (Winter 1997): pp. 43–44. Published in German.

Martin Beck: Putting a face on something is a very powerful representational tool, which is very different from the representational tools of the late 1980s and early 1990s. Public perception of AIDS has shifted from its being an immediate threat to something which is perceived very differently but is still a threat. It has become much more abstract. So visualization and individualizing become tools in themselves.

Julie Ault: The status of representation in relation to needs concerning AIDS is extremely important. Producing a counterrepresentation, as in the late 1980s, no longer works or responds to current conditions. Abstraction or normalization of AIDS is another kind of crisis that has consequences. Also there's a paradox in that a lot of people think there's a cure now; death rates for American white men are down dramatically, but there are obviously many facets to that picture, as well as many other pictures we don't have access to.

John Lindell: One of the problems that I think is critical to the failure of unsafe sex practices is that there have been two contradicting needs and tendencies: to make people with AIDS not seem like spot-ridden lepers who are going to lead a miserable life but to normalize them, increase their personal dignity. At the same time, that then removes the little devil that allowed AIDS educators to say, if you don't practice safer sex, you're gonna get sick and die. And it's gonna be really ugly. So now the argument for safer sex is undercut in a way that it makes representation extremely difficult—particularly for a person who has to keep some sort of reminder in his head to practice safer sex. It's also difficult for society at large to know what's happening with the disease. By giving PWAs a sign of dignity and a normalized life, AIDS is sort of eliminated as a threat by becoming invisible.

From "One Foot Inside and the Other Outside," conversation with Martin Beck and John Lindell. In *AIDS Worlds*. Ed. Frank Wagner, p. 49. Bern: AIDS Info Doc, 1998.

Wong constructs complex pictorial spaces often layered with compartments embedded within other spaces, or layered with language and symbolic systems. Consider, for instance, *Attorney Street: Handball Court with Autobiographical Poem by Piñero* (1982–84). In this intricately composed painting, several communication systems of symbols and signage are nested within one another: the [Miguel] Piñero poem is handprinted in the top part of the painting, where it hovers above a group of tenement buildings; in front of the buildings, a handball court is pictured on which graffiti writers have overlaid tags. Floating in the foreground are seventy-five stylized hands in different positions that presumably spell out the poem penned by Piñero. Surrounding this scene is a border of bricks. The painting is in turn framed by a wooden construction carved on the top part with more signing hands spelling out the title and that the work was "rendered in paint by Martin Wong."

This piece makes us think about language, multiple modes of expression and their translatability, or lack thereof. This painting asks, What are the distinctions between various codes, what do particular codes embody and engender, and how does language define, bond, and bound a community? What are the relations between spoken and written language, sign language, graffiti language, pictorial language, the codes of painting, and so on, ad infinitum? A phrase in the poem, "the code of crime," suggests interpreting behavior and social conditions also as language. Sign language as a recurrent motif for the desire to communicate is utilized by Wong as a metaphor for painting itself.

From "Spaces in Paintings and in Museums: Julie Ault on *Sweet Oblivion: The Urban Landscapes of Martin Wong*. New Museum, New York." *Texte zur Kunst*, no. 31 (September 1998): pp. 176–79. Published in German.

Julie Ault: For many arts organizations operating alongside but distinct from commercial enterprises, a dependency on national and state public funding was produced. Sponsorship constructs and entails an authority-ridden dynamic within which the more powerful element not only determines the terms and rules of exchange but wields punishment and reward respectively as weaponry and control.

The guidelines set by funding agencies determine on an everyday level what kinds of entities are formed, how and whether or not they're maintained and tend to determine the field by imposing certain conventions, procedures, and operating practices that might better be determined contextually. My point is to highlight this exchange, not to make a simplistic value judgment about it. I'm not suggesting to throw all guidelines out and "just let artists be free" but that the dynamics and dependencies produced within the public-funding mix require scrutiny on many levels and, from our perspectives working in the field, not only by congressional oversight.

Jorge Ribalta: I think there is a risk in what you say, that of an oversimplification of the opposition art market versus public realm. You differentiate nonprofit and for profit. This opposition is problematic and complex, and you are aware of it. But, even if you relativize but affirm the connection between nonprofit and for profit, you seem to define the art-market system as a rather conformist site, where critical, socially conscious statements are quite impossible. Thus, you seem to argue that this kind of critique is only possible in alternative, noncommercial structures, and it is linked to nonobjectual practices. I think this can drive to a too simplistic description. Here I go back to one of the central concepts I used in my questions: public service. I think this concept is useful for putting the ideas of profit (non- or for) in wider and more clearly political terms.

JA: It is not my intention to affirm an inherent opposition
between object making and nonobjectual practices or between
marketplaces and not-for-profit enterprises but to differentiate
the overall field accordingly while simultaneously highlighting
interconnections, interdependencies, and overlaps. It's slippery
territory obviously because such differentiations are not solid or
impermeable. I do not subscribe to naive illusions like "artist-
run" and "nonprofit" are by definition of value and critical, and
the market is overdetermined and by definition contaminated.

From interview by Jorge Ribalta. In *Servicio Público: Conversationes sobre finan-
ciación pública y arte contemporáneo.* Ed. Jorge Ribalta, pp. 141–42. Salamanca:
Ediciones Universidad de Salamanca, 1998. Published in Spanish.

Frequently, exhibition apparatuses are made for temporary use. Despite the temporal aspect of such structures, they are designed to support and embellish the actual objects and information being exhibited whether they be art, artifacts, or a new line of products. Whether to entertain, educate, or promote, exhibitions confer value on particular objects and concepts, and value systems are evoked. When an exhibition ends, the support and design structures may be broken down for materials, rearranged for other spatial conditions, or disposed of altogether. Disposable exhibits differ radically insofar as they are both object and framework. Disposability is incongruous with notions of worth.

From "Building and Unbuilding." In *Covering the Room: 8 Ausstellungsflächen*. Ed. Matthias Dusini and Florian Pumhösl, p. 45. Salzburg: Salzburger Kunstverein, 1998. Published in German.

A budget is priorities made concrete.

From "Dear Friend of the Arts." In *Art Matters: How the Culture Wars Changed America*. Ed. Brian Wallis, Marianne Weems, and Philip Yenawine, p. 33. New York: New York University Press, 1999.

The expansion of the art market in the 1980s and the escalation of attacks on public subsidy for culture since 1989 should be understood not as two disparate processes that are merely chronologically coincidental but as interconnected and overlapping forces. In the 1980s, representations of art and artists in entertainment and news media emphasized the monetary value of art and the art industry's embrace of promotional culture. Mainstream media reported and reproduced derogatory glamorizations, which rendered art superficial in the public imagination. Such media representations contributed to the conditions against which congressional forces effectively initiated their agenda to "get the government out of culture," thereby leaving art to prove itself, or not, in the marketplace of ideas. In the late 1980s, critiques and campaigns against public cultural funding trafficked in the demonization of art as well as artists: portraying the art field at best as elitist and at worst as a moral threat to American society. The art market's crash in 1990 and its persistent sluggishness since have functioned effectively as a backdrop for the sustained denigration of contemporary art by politicians and religious fundamentalists.

From "Endtroduction." In *Art Matters: How the Culture Wars Changed America.* Ed. Brian Wallis, Marianne Weems, and Philip Yenawine, p. 251. New York: New York University Press, 1999.

The exhibition structure of *alt.youth.media* and its spatialization
encouraged particular kinds of experience: one might sit, as
I did on numerous occasions, and listen to music, watch TV,
leaf through publications, and scan the room all at once. This
reminded me of how I normally experience culture at home and
in public, flipping from one medium to another, interconnecting
and layering things onto one another. The installation itself did
not suggest a linear or otherwise clear path but encouraged
cross-referencing and making one's own way through. A criticism of "adolescent directionless"[21] was leveled at the exhibition
by one commentator. This critique speaks of people's expectations and reliance on "the clearly marked path," as opposed to
multiple paths, and on intermittent wall texts and other common
features intended to situate viewers and tell them what their relation should be to the objects and materials shown.

Museums generally promote compartmentalizations of culture according to medium. That various media were not segre-
gated from one another but were integrated into a synthesized
environment was a significant effectivity of the exhibition. This
synthesized environment was more akin to the source culture the
materials came from: the display intelligently mirrored the larger
social condition of media culture. In part because *alt.youth.media*
was realized through discursive means and collaborations that
included young cultural producers, it was a rare occasion when
the usual modus operandi museums employ when dealing with
"marginalized or subcultural" practices and products didn't
utterly neutralize and distort the contents.

From "Exhibition: Entertainment, Practice, Platform." In *Agenda, Perspektiven
kritischer Kunst* [*Agenda: Perspectives of Critical Art*]. Ed. Christian Kravagna,
p. 182. Vienna: Folio Verlag, 2000. Published in German.

[21] Howard Halle, "Tonic Youth," *Time
Out*, September 18–25, 1996.

Power Up: Sister Corita and Donald Moffett, Interlocking is a three-way dialogue in the form of an exhibition. . . . Sister Corita, later known as simply Corita, was a Catholic nun who lived and worked in Los Angeles for thirty years. She reached a wide audience with her popular silk-screen prints and engaging style of expressing her views on faith, art, and society. Donald Moffett is a New York City–based artist who emerged in the context of the AIDS crisis. As activist, artist, and designer, Moffett has broadly contributed to the gay-liberation and AIDS-activist movements. Moffett works in a variety of media and uses various modes of distribution in order to engage diverse audiences. My background as an artist has essentially been in collaborative processes of exhibition making engaged with interrelationships between culture and politics. My role in this project is organizing *Power Up*. I regard conceptualizing the exhibition's structure and designing its aesthetic atmosphere as an artistic practice, the exhibition as a medium.

From *Power Up: Sister Corita and Donald Moffett, Interlocking*, n.p. Los Angeles: UCLA Hammer Museum, 2000. Exhibition brochure.

Corita's visual processes were informed by a rather rigid distinction between the content and the aesthetic aspects of artworks. In Baylis Glascock's documentary film *On Teaching and Celebration* (1986), she advises her students "never to start a project with a content-driven idea, but to focus first on shapes and colors or whatever visually interests them, which then—in the process of engagement—would naturally produce content." Although her prints seem to exemplify a more integrated approach to the problematic opposition of form and content, some of the conceptual tools she used to generate them illustrate how decontextualization and recontextualization functioned as productive forces for her printmaking.

Key to her process of decontextualization is a simple tool, a look-through rectangle called a "finder," a device that "helps take things out of context, allows [us] to see for the sake of seeing, and enhances our quick-looking and decision-making skills." Corita's finder can be an empty slide frame, a cut piece of cardboard, or a camera. Using it as a cropping device, as an instrument to look at the world, she points it at various surfaces, from magazine page to cityscape to her own prints. By excluding everything around it, the finder decontextualizes what it finds, and, in Corita's words, allows for "[viewing] life without being distracted by content. You can make visual decisions—in fact, they are made for you."

From Julie Ault and Martin Beck, "All You Need Is Love: Pictures, Words and Worship by Corita Kent." *Eye* 35, no. 9 (Spring 2000): p. 53.

Widely Spaced at Eye Level

Most cultural disciplines and forms of expression have had their structures critiqued, their conventions contested, and their agendas debated in recent decades. Although the curatorial discipline has lagged behind, during the past few years curating has become a subject of critical debate in the art world in the form of conferences, panel discussions, and publications. Concurrently, curatorial training—itself a relatively new branch of study—is being institutionalized in several programs in the US and in European countries. Commonly perceived as an unobtrusive activity, the political functions of curating have been effectively concealed by the assumption of objectivity attached to the practice. A shift is now in process in terms of how curatorial activities and the methods they employ are understood. While curatorial practice is increasingly acknowledged as a form of cultural production, examination of display practices is notably absent from curatorial discourse. Remarkably little literature exists on the topics of installation design and display methodology. What does exist is primarily of the how-to genre, dealing with the practicalities of exhibition making from technical perspectives that treat the form as a pseudoscience.

The Power of Display: A History of Exhibition Installations at the Museum of Modern Art, written by Mary Anne Staniszewski and published by MIT Press (1998), is a welcome and substantial contribution to the field. Staniszewski addresses the noted absence in her introduction: "this book sets out to deal with an aspect of modern art history that has been, generally speaking, officially and collectively forgotten—installation design as an aesthetic medium and historical category." Crucial to the significance of Staniszewski's investigation is her starting position, which considers installation design as medium rather than accessory. Taking installation design as her subject for analysis and the modern art institution—embodied by the Museum of Modern Art (MoMA)—as her object of study, Staniszewski produces a well-researched, informative, and insightfully analytic account of installation practices at MoMA. With considerable editorial and expository skill, Staniszewski traces the historical trajectories of modern installation practices, their causal contexts, and their various impacts on art and on viewers.

The Power of Display is divided into six chapters. The first, "Framing Installation Design: The International Avant-Gardes," constructs a scaffolding of experimental models from which to then investigate MoMA as a case study of diverse installation practices enacted between 1929 and 1970. The chapter contains pictorial and textual histories from key, innovative exhibitions generated by Frederick Kiesler, El Lissitzky, Herbert Bayer, Lilly Reich, and Alexander Dorner.

Chapter two, "Aestheticized Installations for Modernism, Ethnographic Art, and Objects of Everyday Life," is of particular interest. Within this section, Staniszewski charts the installation methods which MoMA's founding director Alfred Barr fashioned beginning in 1929 for the presentation of modern art—what she terms "aestheticized installation for the idealized viewer." With the exception of spare modern installations of the collections in the Hanover Landesmuseum and exhibitions at the Folkwang Museum in Essen—both contemporaneous with Barr—previous installation of art and artifacts utilized salon or skied hanging schemes in decorative, period-room settings. Staniszewski tells how Alfred Barr's desire to aid modern art's legibility led him, contrary to prevailing procedures, to rethink its installation. Taking his cues from the particular features, problematics, and circumstances of modern art, Barr derived the principles to construct an appropriate viewing context. He sought to neutralize the exhibition environment by covering the walls with natural-color cloth upon which he installed artworks at just below eye level with widely spaced intervals. The result was to reinforce the artwork's status as autonomous—from other artworks and from society—and to encourage the viewer's appreciation of the distinct work of art. Through ample spacing of works and by not stacking paintings on top of one another, Barr's installations made it possible for a viewer to experience a one-to-one relationship with each artwork. In keeping with modernist ideals, the viewer was not treated as a social subject but as an autonomous individual. Barr developed his display methods in the context of the newly founded museum, an educational institution whose mission was to advocate modern art to new, broader audiences—the general public. One underlying motive for neutralizing the exhibition space—parallel to an inclination evidenced in abstract painting—was to symbolically detach art from its bourgeois history. In the case of installation design, this also meant disassociating from bourgeois interior design and architecture. Upon considering the historical narrative Staniszewski recounts, what is striking is that modernist installation treatment—now standard practice in museums—was originally an experimental and critical response to then-current conventions.

Chapters three and four, "Installations for Good Design and Good Taste" and "Installations for Political Persuasion," enumerate how purpose generated particularized installation environments and in turn encouraged particular relationships between viewers and artifacts. Staniszewski analyzes several propaganda exhibitions MoMA realized in conjunction with the US government, such as *Road to Victory* (1942), *Airways to Peace* (1943), and Edward Steichen's *The Family of Man* (1955). How these exhibitions ideologically instrumentalized photography in carefully narrativized spaces is discussed in detail.

The book's final sections, "Installation Design and Installation Art" and "The Museum and the Power of Memory," are relatively weak in comparison with what precedes. Chapter five contains valuable information about artists' protests of the museum in the late 1960s, notably Art Workers' Coalition and Guerrilla Art Action Group. The *Information* exhibition of

Conceptual art staged at MoMA in 1970 is also discussed. But the topics of installation and display do not drive Staniszewski's research and writing as forcefully as in earlier sections of the book. What Staniszewski calls "MoMA's laboratory period" eventually gave way to the institutionalization of modern art along with its installation methods. Speaking about MoMA specifically, she concludes: "Certainly the decrease in installation experimentation that took place in the 1960s and 1970s has been in part the result of the consolidation of conventions within modern art museums and is linked to institutionalization of contemporary and modern art and the development of convenient professional formulas." Unfortunately she does not provide description or deeper analysis into the process of institutionalization as it occurred at MoMA. Nor does she discuss the various reinstallations of the permanent collection—itself somewhat of an installation laboratory under the guidance of Kirk Varnedoe in recent years.

As a whole, *The Power of Display* is an impressive archaeology project which brings to light otherwise ephemeral histories from the archival vaults of the Museum of Modern Art. Staniszewski provides readers with an in-depth analysis of the conditions in which modern display practices originated and evolved. These recovered histories reveal the contextual nature of installation practice, thereby challenging the widespread current adaptation of modernist display modes with some tough questions. What is being promoted and simultaneously excluded through broad adherence to modernist-style presentation methods? Does this usage express nostalgia for modernism? What kind of relations between art, artist, and audience are generated in such installation frameworks? What kind of relations between art, artist, and audience might be generated from differing approaches?

The republication of Brian O'Doherty's long out-of-print *Inside the White Cube: The Ideology of the Gallery Space* by the University of California Press (1999) makes accessible another significant text which is helpful in deciphering the sociopolitical-aesthetic underpinnings of display modes of modern and contemporary art. Although it was written in 1976, artist O'Doherty's vivid, insightful, and idiosyncratic account of how modern painting left the easel and entered galleries and museums—and with what implications—is more relevant than ever. O'Doherty locates ideology in the codification of modernist display practice, which he regards as an interlocking development of the reproduction of the gallery space as white cube—a space which seeks to transcend specificity of time and location. O'Doherty states early in the first chapter: "Hanging, indeed, is what we need to know more about. From Courbet on, conventions of hanging are an unrecovered history. The way pictures are hung makes assumptions about what is offered. Hanging editorializes on matters of interpretation and value, and is unconsciously influenced by taste and fashion."

O'Doherty interprets the modernist gallery as "aesthetic chamber," as "icon of modernism," as "value system," and as "context." Through various filters he analyzes its effects on art and on viewers. O'Doherty regards the white cube as a context that ultimately unifies the art industry and its participants in elitist communion: "For many of us, the gallery space still gives off negative vibrations when we wander in. Esthetics are tuned into a kind of social elitism—the gallery space is *exclusive*. Isolated in plots of space, what is on display looks a bit like valuable scarce goods, jewelry, or silver: esthetics are turned into commerce—the gallery space is *expensive*. What it contains is, without initiation, well-nigh incomprehensible—art is *difficult*. Exclusive audience, rare objects difficult to comprehend—here we have a social, financial, and intellectual snobbery which models our system of limited production, our modes of assigning value, our social habits at large. Never was a space, designed to accommodate the prejudices and enhance the self-image of the upper middle classes, so efficiently codified."

O'Doherty draws on many artists' works and strategies, notably Marcel Duchamp, William Anastasi, and Claes Oldenburg, to explain by example relationships of art and artists to the gallery space. But *Inside the White Cube* is not an art-historical text. Rather it is a hybrid form made from a mixture of empirical, analytic, academic, and journalistic methods. *Inside the White Cube* is in part a critique of "the economic model of art as product." For O'Doherty, art as "portable currency" necessitates the stripped-down, controlled context of the white cube: art and context are understood to be conjoined, mutually producing one another.

The white-cube-style space, as well as modernist-style installation design, are descendants of strategies used to produce exhibition contexts for modern art—strategies that were originally devised through curatorial engagement with the circumstances of exhibiting particular art at a particular time. In museum and gallery culture, particularly in the US, the white cube—with variances—continues to be a favored architectural setting for contemporary art exhibitions. It provides an idealized environment distinct from the referential space of society. In the contemporary art space the systematic stripping away of anything that might connect art to social processes and the world outside is common practice. Devoid of decoration, windows, seating, or other furniture, and of course whitened with paint, according to O'Doherty, white-cube-style spaces are "constructed along laws as rigorous as those for building a medieval church." The ubiquity of such spaces renders them nearly invisible, thereby consolidating their power to reinforce and reproduce existing power configurations. One thing is clear: the white-cube-style space as a reproducible apparatus serves a cultural economy in which art is defined by its status as marketable product.

On a parallel track, modernist-style display continues to be widely favored as an installation mode for contemporary art. Many exhibitions deploy a museological mode of display, which assigns genius to the artist and masterpiece status to the curated artworks. The presenting institution—whether it be a gallery, a kunsthalle, or a museum—considers and promotes itself as

arbiter of superiority. The viewer is offered a relatively passive
role as witness. These interlocking goals are articulated through
the theatricals of spatialization, lighting, wall texts, and other
devices. In such a setup, artworks are hung at widely spaced
intervals and at just below median eye level.

Why do some practices become convention over others? It is
doubtful that the sustained proliferation of the white-cube-style
space in tandem with modernist-style display represents simple
laziness. More likely, adherence to these—as conventions—
represents resistance to rethinking the terms of art after modernism. Display methods developed in specific museum contexts
(i.e., Barr at MoMA) have perhaps been adopted by curators,
gallerists, and artists, not only to appropriate and invoke the aura
of the museum but to distinguish art from common goods. As
contemporary art has become more and more institutionalized,
and the art industry has increasingly consolidated as a marketplace, distinguishing art from other products is perhaps viewed
as a necessary strategy to protect its historical, symbolic value as
a cultural category. In opposition to the crowded, repetition-
based arrangements of the common supermarket, spaciousness
communicates symbolic value and the authority of uniqueness.
The amount of wall real estate awarded an artwork signifies
value and position within the hierarchical logic system of the
art industry. The sheer volume of white-cube-style spaces narrativized by modernist origins and display techniques suggests a
nostalgia for, and allegiance to, modernism at large in the art world.
Similarly, conventional display modes, which treat art and artifacts
as autonomous, generic examples of a medium, i.e., photography
or painting, can be interpreted as representative of a longing for
clear-cut divisions between mediums.

Exhibitions are key intersections where art and artifacts are made
available to audiences, within which narratives, ideas, and sensations are activated. It is precisely because of the power that exhibitions and display have in assigning, determining, or opening up

meanings that modernist-style installation convention needs to be challenged. The notion that content can simply be inserted into existing exhibition and display forms as though those forms were neutral, or as though artistic production were generic, is deeply problematic. Art is at risk of being confined by its presentation rather than expanded and suitably contextualized. What might appear as an expansive and reverential installation, while entirely appropriate for some artworks (modern or otherwise), is inappropriate for others. What Staniszweski calls "convenient professional formulas," applied indiscriminately, may have a distorting effect. Installation convention can neutralize and objectify vital artistic practices and related social processes.

Adherence to conventions that dictate according to a set of rules and procedures is by definition contradictory to a contextual process. Modernist-style display—as convention—has been institutionalized to the degree where it is taken for granted and seems natural. Yet modernist aestheticized installation was developed through a contextual approach to particular art; principles of display emerged from congruent principles in modern art itself. This model demonstrates how a contextual approach to installation design and display can render solutions that activate art and viewer. But a contextual approach to installation requires presentational modes to be considered mutable and contingent. It implies approaching the activities of installation design and display anew in relation to particular contents, materials, and circumstances. The challenge is to fashion presentational environments that take into account not only the context(s) the artworks/practices derived from but also the context being constructed in an exhibition. Alternative exhibition strategies that defy convention and propose contextual approaches potentially challenge the very categorizations and hierarchies by which relations in the art industry are reproduced.

Despite the ubiquity of modernist-style display conventions, innovation and intervention in the field of installation design is ongoing. There are countless artists and curators throughout

modern and recent art history who have utilized display to rup-
ture the pretense of installation neutrality. As curatorial and
installation practices diversify, and related discourse expands,
one hopes that investigations of key alternative installation and
display practices—particularly those produced by artists—will
be committed to print with insight and analytic facility equal
to that evidenced in both *The Power of Display* and *Inside the
White Cube*.

Springerin 6, no. 1 (Spring 2000): pp. 38–42. Published in German.

OS, id was laid out as a series of overlapping arenas suggested by density and content, composed with preexisting as well as newly produced materials. For example, the arena entitled *grid* included a table designed in 1970 by the Italian collective Superstudio. On the table, plexiglass sign holders contained information about Superstudio's *Supersurface* project, one manifestation of which is the table's gridded laminate surface. The table was itself situated in front of an outdoor-size vinyl billboard showing a photograph we shot in 1999 of an uninhabited California desert landscape that nonetheless is marked by street signs as the intersection of Avenue D and 170th Street. This coordinate within the territory that has long since been mapped in anticipation of capitalist development was juxtaposed with a video monitor that continuously showed Superstudio's 1972 film *Supersurface: An Alternative Model for Life on the Earth*. Also integrated within this arena were aerial photographs of sprawling suburban residential developments that we commissioned from a Los Angeles–based photographer. Finally, panels with images and texts on the adjacent walls provided information about Superstudio and their conceptual project *12 Ideal Cities*.

In such ways, historical and contemporary elements could be read in varied forms and arrangements as a network of interconnected references to assist viewers in simultaneously making connections and grasping the contradictions between, for example, the utopian underpinnings of Superstudio's grid project and the dystopian facts of suburban land development. Viewers could engage with the dialogue of images, objects, texts, and sounds in an environment in which interpretation was neither predetermined nor prematurely foreclosed.

From Julie Ault and Martin Beck, *Outdoor Systems, indoor distribution*, n.p. Ed. Julie Ault and Martin Beck. Berlin: Neue Gesellschaft für bildende Kunst (nGbK), 2000. Exhibition catalogue.

Most art institutions have standardized procedures for doing
things. Coming up against those procedures with alternative
modes and alternative agendas—from selecting and developing
a subject and a structure for an exhibition, to what information
one includes in the text of a press release, to the display techniques by which art and artifacts are presented—in my experience invariably presents conflicts. Every detail in the process
of making an exhibition, from the initial conceptualizing of its
structure and scope to negotiation with staff at the institution
which presents and finances it, is imbued with politics—on the
everyday procedural level as well as in the larger context of cultural politics. Specific political conflicts relevant to a project's
particular subject matter may also emerge. Nearly every exchange
that takes place within the making of a project has eventual consequences for viewers, and I regard nearly every exchange as an
aspect of my practice.

I didn't choose my practice from a list of existing possibilities
but developed it over time, primarily in the context of Group
Material and the larger politicized milieu of 1980s and 1990s cultural activism in New York. For the purpose of this discussion,
I am trying to articulate the features and goals of that practice,
but I have to add that I don't consider it to be fixed or formulaic.
I work contextually, and a contextual approach means the material criteria and methodologies employed are contingent upon
purpose, location, material parameters, and the issues at stake.

From "Exhibition as Political Space." In *Dürfen die das?* [*Are They Allowed To Do
That?*]. Ed. Stella Rollig and Eva Sturm, p. 53. Vienna: Verlag Turia + Kant, 2002.

Alternative Art New York, 1965–1985 consists of four intermingled layers of information: texts, images, documents, and a chronology of alternative structures. The book recounts and analyzes histories from multiple perspectives. It is informed by my experience of working collaboratively in this very field and is commensurate with its dialogic foundation. To convey histories, especially those emerging from philosophies of self-representation and cultural civil rights, is a challenge best met by assembling a group of writers who employ different methodologies and styles to investigate their diverse topics with intellectual rigor. One tenet of the alternative arts movement has been the merit of dislodging restrictive categorizations and hierarchies (of mediums, of types of cultural practice, and of identity structures). Bringing together investigatory methods and writing styles that ordinarily are not joined—academic, journalistic, empirical, and hybrids—supports that principle.

From "For the Record." In *Alternative Art New York, 1965–1985*. Ed. Julie Ault, p. 11. Minneapolis: University of Minnesota Press; New York: Drawing Center, 2002.

The formation of ABC No Rio was an unplanned consequence of the *Real Estate Show* staged by a group of artists at the end of the 1970s. Alan Moore, Ann Messner, Rebecca Howland, Christy Rupp, Bobby G., and others illegally occupied an abandoned building at 123 Delancey Street and mounted an exhibition about property and housing. Calculated to highlight the warehousing of space practiced by the City of New York, the occupation attracted the attention of officials from the Department of Housing, Preservation, and Development. Suspecting the seizure might be part of a well-planned political initiative, these authorities swiftly reclaimed the building and confiscated the exhibition. The *Real Estate Show* initiators negotiated to reopen it. Newspaper coverage was sympathetic to the artists' plight, and the Department of Housing, Preservation, and Development, wanting to escape further bad publicity, offered the group an alternate site in the neighborhood. That storefront at 156 Rivington Street was to be rent-free for two years and "affordable" thereafter. The crude space was dubbed ABC No Rio (inspired by the remaining legible letters of a nearby sign) and its operation as an arts and community center began.

From "A Chronology of Selected Alternative Structures, Spaces, Artists' Groups, and Organizations in New York City, 1965–1985." In *Alternative Art New York, 1965–1985*. Ed. Julie Ault, p. 59. Minneapolis: University of Minnesota Press; New York: Drawing Center, 2002.

Archives in Practice

Frances Elizabeth Kent was born in 1918 to an Irish Catholic family. Upon completing her Catholic education, Frances entered the Immaculate Heart of Mary Religious Community in Los Angeles and took the name Sister Mary Corita. Between 1938 and 1968 Sister Corita lived and worked in the communal environment of the Immaculate Heart Community (IHC) and its college.

In 1962, Pope John XXIII's Vatican II decree on the "Adaptation and Renewal of Religious Life" called for movement toward modern values, including fewer restrictions on nuns' daily lives, and a new focus on social action and service. In her art, and in her capacity as teacher and chair of the college's art department from 1964 to 1968, Sister Corita, who was also known simply as Corita, embodied the modern nun. Corita reached a wide audience with her popular silk-screen prints and engaging style of expressing her views on faith, art, and society. In her work from the 1960s, she quoted advertising slogans and mimicked package-design motifs; she appropriated the colors of the marketplace and the aesthetics of commercial culture to ground her religious and political messages in contemporary urban life. Corita left her order in 1969 and moved to Boston, where she lived until her death in 1986.

Corita's primary art medium was printmaking. Her editions were generally unnumbered, produced in quantities ranging from a few to a few hundred. Throughout her thirty-five-year career, during which she frequently instructed her students to "save everything," Corita kept one example of nearly each of the prints she made. Her personal collection also contained printed materials including her writings and correspondence; publicity such as invitation cards, posters, and press clippings; publications she made or contributed to; references and sources used in her art including advertisements, bumper stickers, and political buttons; and a photographic repository consisting of thousands of slides she had taken.

Corita made provisions for her collection to be divided into two parts after her death. Her will specified that the respective accumulations should enter two Los Angeles institutions. The examples of her serigraphs—what amounted to more than nine hundred prints as well as related drawings and sketchbooks—were donated for posterity to the foremost works-on-paper archive in the city, the Grunwald Center for the Graphic Arts at the University of California at Los Angeles (UCLA). The second body, consisting largely of her remaining inventory of prints and watercolors she made in the 1970s and '80s, was bequeathed to the IHC. Her will stipulated these artworks were to be for sale and that proceeds should support her brother as well as benefit the IHC. Slides and printed materials were likewise left to the IHC.

The IHC is visited mostly by its Catholic members and affiliates, while the Grunwald Center is primarily utilized by scholars and historians. Both institutions embody values—community, renewal, tradition, preservation—which were meaningful to Corita. Her decision to preserve one body of material in a proper archive and to distribute the other through the context of her spiritual community provides some insights into her thinking as well as sheds light on the functions and uses of archives.

Relevant to the subject of contemporary art practice and archives, following are some thoughts on my experiences while engaging with Corita's work inside the two institutions, and some reflections on the interpretations of Corita's art practice that the collections engendered. Alongside are thoughts on how I presented my research in a public exhibition format, by including particular information and by using a distinct approach to display.

In 1995 I had only a vague awareness of Corita Kent. That year I had received one of her prints as a gift. The bold composition, entitled *o is for o my god* (1968), made me want to know more. I quickly found a book Corita had illustrated and a couple of articles on her work, one of which contained a reproduction of a print composed of primary-colored disc shapes titled *wonderbread* (1962). The idea of a Catholic nun appropriating iconography from package design was intriguing and full of promise.

I learned from the article that Corita had lived at the IHC in Los Angeles so I gave them a call. Upon hearing of my interest, Sister Stephanie Baxter, the woman in charge of the collection, assured me I would be welcome to visit. A few weeks later I encountered the extraordinary. Inside of flat files stored in a small room adorned with Corita's work were hundreds of her prints, one more exciting than the next for its graphic composition and complex content. That such an inventive and significant body of work was neither celebrated in the art world nor historicized in the art-history field seemed remarkable. Adding to my amazement was that I was seeing it in a Catholic community center and not in a museum.

I informed Sister Stephanie of my desire to work toward displaying Corita's prints in an upcoming exhibition I was organizing. The exhibition, then in the planning stage, was to be a juxtaposition of graphic, media, and artworks by Donald Moffett with another artist. Upon seeing her prints, I immediately decided the appropriate pairing would be with Corita. Sister Stephanie was enthusiastic and gave me unrestricted access to Corita's archive. She promised that next time I could look in the basement, where more prints were stored.

Subsequent visits to the IHC were equally exciting as the first. The basement contained another treasure trove, including prints that were not duplicated upstairs. I was left on my own to spend hours going through piles of works, taking notes, and looking through related ephemeral materials such as press clippings and publications as well as the artist's extensive slide collection. This rich photographic repository includes images exemplary of Corita's ongoing process of looking through the camera for stimulus—photographs taken in supermarkets, on the street, and at exhibitions and fairs; pictures she took of her travels; and documentation of IHC events including the Mary Day processions choreographed under her guidance.

My experiences visiting the IHC were infused with Corita's presence; her spirit seemed to be a tangible force there. Many of her prints as well as photographs of Corita hung on the walls of every room in the building. She was frequently spoken about and her creative principles referenced by the women who worked there as part of everyday conversation. The informal conversations I had with those women, many of whom had been Corita's colleagues, were fortifying, as was the communal spirit. This was clearly a living archive.

Sister Stephanie, who had been a contemporary of Corita, retired in 1997. She was replaced by Peggy Kayser, a museum professional from outside the community. Peggy was enlisted to administrate the collection and to bring Corita's work into current public exposure. Peggy's agenda included setting up an accurate database of the collection and housing the prints in archival protection. In order to build a comprehensive archive of Corita's works, she sought out examples of prints that were not already in the IHC's holdings. Until then, artist's proofs and last examples of editions had been sold (not irresponsibly but in keeping with Corita's will) rather than saved. Since the 1960s, the silkscreens had been priced between $25 and $300. Peggy also raised the prices to a more reasonable market value. She formalized what had been an informal collection into an entity called the Corita Art Center.

One day in 1999, while I was discussing Corita with Peggy, she mentioned that perhaps some of the gaps I'd found in the IHC's collection might be filled in by a visit to the Grunwald Center for the Graphic Arts. This was the first time that anyone mentioned this part of the archive to me. I'd been researching

Corita for three years (and already had mounted an exhibition in 1997) and had never come across this crucial fact.[1]

The Grunwald Center for the Graphic Arts at UCLA preserves and conserves paper, specifically prints, drawings, photographs, and artists' books, from the sixteenth century to the present. The center makes its holdings available for individual and scholarly use and occasionally mounts exhibits. According to hearsay, Corita had a casual conversation in the mid-1960s with a UCLA professor in charge of the Grunwald, during which either he suggested or she offered that her collection of serigraphs eventually be donated to the center. Twenty years later, without any further discussion or any formal agreement, Corita specified the gift for the Grunwald in her will.[2] Also according to rumor, the gatekeepers of the Grunwald Center didn't readily agree that Corita's life's work should become the institution's responsibility.

Corita regarded printmaking as: "a very democratic form, since it enables me to produce a quantity of original art for those who cannot afford to purchase high-priced art." While Corita had scores of admirers throughout her career, her artwork did not primarily circulate in the fine-art system, nor had it ever achieved "fine-art" status in the eyes of many professional curators, art critics, and historians. Corita rejected what she perceived as an elitist distribution system. Her large editions

---

[1] The original exhibition I organized that included Corita's work was titled *Power Up: Reassembled Speech, Interlocking Sister Corita and Donald Moffett* and took place at the Wadsworth Atheneum in Hartford, Connecticut, in 1997. An expanded version of that exhibition retitled *Power Up: Sister Corita and Donald Moffett, Interlocking* was made for the UCLA Hammer Museum in Los Angeles in 2000.

[2] The reported conversation was not her only exchange with UCLA. Corita had various associations with UCLA over time; on occasion she lectured in the art department, she staged exhibitions there, which she had produced with her IHC students, and she participated in an oral-history project conducted by the Department of History, which documented cultural figures of Los Angeles in 1976.

of silkscreens were deliberately priced inexpensively. Although some prints were sold from galleries, including one called Corita Prints that she and her sister, Mary Downey, opened in Santa Monica specifically to do so, they were also sold from churches, community centers, and even vans driven by IHC members to various cultural and religious gatherings.

Having been unsuccessful at locating documentation on the matter I can't accurately state the reasons for the Grunwald's original resistance to her work. But I assume that Corita's Catholicism and her populist attitude—details that potentially marginalized her work in the eyes of the art world—could easily have been cofactors, perhaps in tandem with other institutionally specific concerns. Regardless, within a short period the Grunwald finally agreed to accept the collection for its archive.

The Grunwald is an archival archive within which everything is catalogued and well protected. Its chief responsibility is to conserve and protect its holdings for perpetuity. This requires that the institution maintain a trustworthy security system. Visitors and researchers must be accompanied at all times by a responsible staff member. The director of conservation dictates how and with what frequency materials in the archive can be exposed to public view. Works on paper are particularly vulnerable to light. Therefore, unlike at the IHC, Corita's prints are not hanging on the walls but are stored in darkness.[3]

After getting through the formality of the Grunwald Center, Corita's flat files contained treasure upon treasure. I came across

---

[3.] Lighting issues also emerged when mounting the second version of *Power Up* at the UCLA Hammer Museum (an affiliate of the Grunwald Center for the Graphic Arts) in 2000. Corita's prints selected for exhibition contained a lot of text, sometimes small, and were brightly colored, some with fluorescent inks. The predominance of text along with the bold use of color and composition characteristic to Corita's art seemed to require ample lighting. However, conservation restrictions dictated a much lower light level than desired and produced a reverential and hushed atmosphere distinct from what I originally felt would ideally highlight the works exhibited.

many works I had not been previously aware of, as well as ones
I knew only from reproductions. The collection also contained
numerous variations on compositions, which demonstrated that
Corita recycled ideas. Color patterns, images, texts, and textual
fragments were often reused and recontextualized in relation
to other elements. While the Corita collection housed at the
Grunwald was tremendously exhilarating to explore, I couldn't
help but notice the sharp contrast of that environment to that of
the IHC. The center's sober and bureaucratic milieu seemed an
unlikely match for Corita's artistic legacy, at least on the surface.
But although I was initially sorry to see so much energy, color,
force, and passion lying dormant in the storage facility, were it
not for the Grunwald's conservative attitude and protection, her
works might have prematurely and unnecessarily deteriorated,
or, worse yet, might not even exist any longer.[4]

What foresight influenced Corita's decisions concerning what
should eventually go where and with what conditions? I can only
speculate that as a Catholic, populist, politicized woman printmaker whose artistic legacy was in these ways marginalized in the
mainstream art field, Corita grasped that her life's work was in
danger of disappearance. At stake was the potential for her work
to be engaged, studied, interpreted, and written about in the
future. Finding institutions that would and could permanently
care for her art and artifacts—and that had the authority to
confer historical legitimacy on her practice—was crucial for
its conservation.

Specific narratives about people, society, and history take
shape from using an archive depending on what is contained

4. According to records, the Grunwald's
Corita collection has not been frequently consulted nor had any of it
been exhibited between her death in
1986 and 1999, when I approached
the institution to stage *Power Up*
at the UCLA Hammer Museum.
The center's curatorial staff was very
enthusiastic about the opportunity
to exhibit Corita's works from their
collection, particularly in relation to
more recent work of a contemporary
artist.

therein. Interpretation is influenced by what is looked at or studied, and with what filters and expectations. Because they are repositories of documents or "facts," archives seem to tell the truth, and they do so with a degree of authority. Archives tell truths, but they can also "lie" through omission or mislead. Connecting the dots between discrete documents and discovering relations between information—producing meaning—is what is at the heart of research. But the "facts" housed within a particular archive are not necessarily systematic. They are often fragmentary, disconnected from context, and sometimes even random. Crucial pieces of information which might answer questions, suggest particular narratives, or unlock mysteries are not necessarily archived.[5]

Both the IHC and the Grunwald Center are capable of telling different stories about Corita's work, by way of what is included as well as what is excluded in the respective collections. For example, the Grunwald archive, though seemingly complete as it contains one of nearly each of her prints, depicts Corita's artistic practice through the relatively coherent, enduring form of art objects. But even taken as a whole, her prints provide only a partial picture. Other interpretations of her artistic practice emerge once the frame of research is expanded to include the IHC ephemera collection. Looking at images such as the ones of the visually dynamic Mary Day processions Corita choreographed

---

[5] Several years ago, out of curiosity, I requested the artist's file under my name at New York City's Museum of Modern Art library. I opened the file to find only one sheet of paper, a letter I had once sent to an art historian who had since donated her papers to the library. I was horrified that this was the sole document that represented me in the context of an important repository about contemporary art. What about the work I had been involved with as an artist that had left a substantial paper trail? Why was that entirely absent while a letter intended to be read by only one person was saved and made accessible publicly? This anecdotal situation provided a glimpse into the ambivalent, nonjudgmental nature of the archive. The experience has since functioned as a cautionary signpost whenever I embark on research.

or at pictures of advertising signage she fragmented through cropping offer an expanded perspective of her creative practice and impact upon understandings of Corita's prints as well. Potentially, such an extended view complicates Corita's artistic practice and output.

Even the site of the archive affects the interpretation of what is archived. Conducting research at the IHC revealed that Corita's work was part of (and due to) a larger context—a creative community environment within which nuns, teachers, students, visitors, and even the media participated. Reading through the inventively designed *Irregular Bulletins* produced by the IHC College's art department (of which Corita had been chair between 1964–68) and reading the many write-ups about IHC activities revealed the complex layers of collaboration at work in the art department, as well as in the making of Corita's prints. Though the signature on the prints was Corita's and she was often singled out in the press as the guiding force and spokesperson for the art department, research showed that her artworks as well as the department's achievements were the results of social and collective processes. Had I for instance only visited the Grunwald Center to learn about Corita's work, I might have accepted her practice at face value as represented within that collection—Corita as visionary printmaker and sole author of the works, an artist whose output seemed coherent and complete therein.[6]

Joining art objects and ephemeral materials within an art exhibition is a curatorial strategy I have employed on various occasions, originally when making thematic exhibitions on the relationship between aesthetics and politics within the

[6.] It is striking that Corita donated her papers and photographic materials to the IHC rather than to the Grunwald. Although the Grunwald is a scholarly institution with the resources to preserve and make such materials accessible for study, Corita probably felt the visual and textual records of collaboration essentially belonged to that community that the documented activities emerged from, and decided to "return" them to their original context.

collaborative Group Material, and later for projects I've organized that deal with historical cultural formations. Combining art with documentary or other forms of ephemeral material in exhibitions can symbolically dislodge the separations between art and ephemera imposed by institutional structures, and redress the hierarchical schematization imposed upon cultural production in which the enduring (i.e., art objects) is sanctioned over the ephemeral (i.e., documents). This strategy is also motivated by desires to recover the ephemeral in order to mine its meanings, uses, and contexts.

Because exhibition space has traditionally been considered an aesthetic domain, contextualizing information (e.g., information about other activities an artist engaged in besides her "primary" practice) is usually relegated to the space of the publication. *Power Up: Sister Corita and Donald Moffett, Interlocking*, staged at the UCLA Hammer Museum in 2000, sought to challenge that division and the commonly held distinctions between "exhibition" and "publication" and between "aesthetics" and "information."[7] Ephemeral materials and information gathered during the research process, deepening my understanding of the artists, their practices, and the periods in which their works were made, were integrated into the exhibition itself. I sought to do so

7. *Power Up: Sister Corita and Donald Moffett, Interlocking* at the UCLA Hammer Museum, Los Angeles, in 2000 was a three-way dialogue in the form of an exhibition. Sister Corita reached a wide audience with her popular silk-screen prints and engaging style of expressing her views on faith, art, and society. Donald Moffett is a New York City–based artist who emerged in the context of the AIDS crisis. As activist, artist, and designer, Moffett has broadly contributed to the gay-liberation and AIDS-activist movements. Moffett works in a variety of media and uses various modes of distribution in order to engage diverse audiences. As the third artist in the dialogue, my role was organizing *Power Up* and designing its aesthetic atmosphere. Conceptual and compositional strategies in Corita's and Moffett's works set the stage for and determined the many particulars of how the exhibition looked. For the purpose of this essay, I am focusing on the aspects of presentation and display in *Power Up* that relate to Corita.

in visually engaging ways using presentational devices that enlivened and suitably contextualized material rather than rendering it rarefied.

Reuniting the ephemeral and the enduring in *Power Up* helped represent a fuller comprehension of Corita's creative practice than if only her prints were exhibited. Access to photographs, documentary materials, quotations from the IHC's collection, and prints, including many that had not been available for the original version of the exhibition from the Grunwald archive, made it possible to bridge the two collections and the stories they tell.[8] Exhibiting ephemeral materials from the IHC also allowed me to demonstrate the collaborative underpinnings of Corita's practice, and to establish that in addition to printmaking, her practice as a whole included book and object making, graphic design, photography, staging events, happenings, making speeches, writing, and teaching.

By design, *Power Up* emphasized itself as a functional arena. To extend the content of the show from the walls into the open space of the room, I used three-dimensional elements, rectilinear box-like forms painted in combinations of white, yellow, light blue, and red. Ascribed with multiple functions, these structures were at once pedestals, platforms, seating, furnishings, sculptural elements, and display surfaces. Photographs, including some of

---

8. Since I did not know about the Grunwald's holdings when I organized the first version of *Power Up*, for that exhibition I relied solely on the IHC. When we discussed the possibility of exhibiting a number of prints, Sister Stephanie told me they were not really set up for loaning and shipping artworks—that it would be best if I bought the pieces for the show, which I did. For the exhibit at the UCLA Hammer Museum, it was clear that rather than use the prints I owned, selections from the Grunwald's collection would be shown, thereby making visible the connection between the archive (the Grunwald Center for the Graphic Arts) and the exhibiting institution (the UCLA Hammer Museum). The Grunwald collection gave me a nearly comprehensive pool to choose from and included key works I had no prior access to, including the four-part print titled *Power Up*, which inspired the exhibition's title.

the Corita-organized Mary's Day processions, and ephemera, such as magazines, flyers, greeting cards, and stickers, were attached to these cube-like seats and platforms. Quotations by Corita ranging from offhanded comments to formal statements on art and society were produced in brightly colored vinyl lettering and adhered to the structures as another layer of commentary. A book made by Corita, *Footnotes and Headlines* (Herder and Herder, New York, 1967), emblematic of her methods of layering texts, was displayed as an object hung on a wall. On the floor nearby, color reproductions of each of the book's page spreads were laid out side by side on top of a large platform, so viewers could have access to the publication's interior.[9] Other books for which Corita designed the jackets, as well as facsimiles of the *Irregular Bulletin*, were laid on top of the platform surface for visitors to look through. Usually in museums, such objects are displayed in vitrines, foreclosing the possibility to look through and handle them as was originally intended.

These furnishings provided a layer of additional forms and of aesthetic information in dialogue with the prints, which were hung on the walls. In this way the prototypical hierarchy within which art is separated from and privileged over contextual materials, regarded as ancillary, was counterbalanced. The furnishings articulated an inclusive space for visitors in the midst of the exhibition. Viewers watching videotapes presented in the exhibition (including one by Baylis Glascock titled *Corita Kent: On Teaching and Celebration* [1986]) or looking at and reading elements of the show were physically situated amidst the exhibit.

Corita's voice, as employed through her artworks, through excerpts of her writings and speech, and through mirroring her methods and style in fashioning the presentational environment, formed layers of aesthetic information, which composed and

---

9. This book was influential for the exhibition specifically since the page layouts and layering of texts had sparked the idea for the paint scheme used in *Power Up*.

guided viewers through the exhibition. The various ephemeral materials that became part of the exhibition expanded the view on and understandings of Corita's art practice, articulated points of identification for visitors already familiar with or who had been directly involved in Corita's milieu, and provided points of entry into various aesthetic and political circumstances, as well as social histories being made available to new viewers.

Historiography, whether done traditionally or with alternative methods and tools, is a creative practice and a form of production, which ultimately embodies the process of uncovering, discovering, and recovering. What is at stake in the discussion is how archives provide access to experience, our own and that of others. Articulations of history—specific conditions, as well as more abstract conceptions of events in time—are produced through such engagements.

The common demarcations we employ to aid our comprehension and articulations of art and culture (categories, disciplines, and labels) are certainly useful, as are systems of measure and categorization, which undeniably make the world more graspable. Official archives have traditionally depended on and embody classification systems while they preserve historical material.

While systems of categorization may help engender comprehension, the resultant legibility may come with a cost. Cultural, social, and historical formations are not very orderly. If my experiences learning about Corita through the two collections within their respective institutional homes can be taken as an example, cultural formations, including that of "the artist," seem to contradict and evade principles of containment.

From *Interarchive: Archival Practices and Sites in the Contemporary Art Field*. Ed. Beatrice von Bismarck, Hans-Peter Feldmann, Hans Ulrich Obrist, Diethelm Stoller, and Ulf Wuggenig, pp. 98–104. Cologne: Walther König; Lüneburg: Kunstraum der Universität Lüneburg, 2002.

After September 11th, New York's cultural institutions were compelled to "do something." Several courted *here is new york*, which seemed the ideal ready-made response—a seemingly apolitical exhibition that includes and attracts large numbers of the public, promoting participation and community. Currently on view is the Museum of Modern Art's exhibition *Life of the City*, which includes photographs from its collection beside snapshots relating to the city derived from an open call and a sampling of *here is new york* presented on a large-scale flat screen. Nearby, in collaboration with the International Center of Photography, an installment of *here is new york* is on view in a donated storefront, titled *history unframed*. A flyer explains, "Our guiding principle is the same as it was six months ago—that if one photograph tells a story, thousands of photographs tell not only thousands of stories but also perhaps can at least begin to tell the story if they are allowed to speak for themselves, to each other, and to the viewer directly, unframed either by glass, metal or wood, or by preconceptions or editorial comment. In the political sphere it is this principle, after all, which America's Founding Fathers advanced when they developed the notion of democracy."

An ad hoc grassroots response to a crisis, *here is new york* appears to be a model of democratic culture. It provided an outlet for people to air images, opinions, and emotions, and considerable money was raised. While the organizers' efforts and intentions are laudable, the projects' extension eight months after the fact seems problematic, in part because underpinning political contexts—previously shrouded by the catastrophe—have come into focus in numerous ways that cannot in good faith be ignored. The curatorially nonjudgmental approach of *here is new york* seemed a logical response within the immediacy of a ground-level crisis, but that the project has not since been rethought is disturbing. Continuing to exhibit sensational and emotionally compelling images—predominantly of the World Trade Center during and after its collapse, victims, and rescuers—functions conservatively. Presented as fact, in the absence of captions, these photographs are readily interpreted along the lines of mainstream-media representations viewers have absorbed, which have trafficked in a mixture of emotional pornography and boosterism for US governmental actions.

From "Öffentlichkeit vermarkten" ["Boosting the American Public"]. *Zitty*, no. 11 (2002): p. 76. Published in German.

I would like to believe that critical alternative activities have permanently altered accepted notions of possible functions and definitions of art. But a casual tour of New York's art spaces, galleries, and museums on any given day of the week does not necessarily support that belief. Clearly the overhaul of the art industry and its social relations posited by many alternative organizations, and lobbied for by numerous individuals and groups, did not happen. Most art institutions are still hierarchically organized with boards composed of preeminent members of high society and finance. Most art institutions have no artists on their boards. Currently, there is little evidence of experimentation, grossly insufficient exposure for unaffiliated artists, curtailed potential for art's infiltration into daily city life and publicly used space, and limited indication of cultural activism by or for artists. Art has not been reconnected to larger society, as was desired by some, or to political and social issues. The art world remains just that—a world unto itself, which operates according to its own values and with its own economic system.

In spite of the alternative arts movement, during much of the 1990s and continuing into the present, the art field is marked by polarization, with "aesthetic" practice (and product) at one end of the spectrum and "the political" at the other. The persistence of such obfuscation is one of the problematic binarisms that the Art Workers' Coalition and many participants in the alternative sphere aimed to disentangle and dislodge, through analysis, protest, dialogue, and example.

From "Alternative New York." In Julie Ault and Martin Beck, *Critical Condition, Selected Texts in Dialogue*. Ed. Marius Babias, p. 314. Essen: Kokerei Zollverein/ Zeitgenössische Kunst und Kritik, 2003.

*12th Session: In the late 1980s, a new kind of cultural activism
coalesced around the AIDS struggle. Can you describe to us the context of Group Material's involvement in these issues?*

Julie Ault: When Group Material started to focus on the AIDS
issue in 1988, many of us had already recognized the extent to
which this disease was affecting our lives. Many of our friends
and intimates had become HIV positive. Surprisingly enough,
by that time, there had been very little discussion on a public
level in the art world concerning AIDS.

The first artist who registered the realities and politics of
AIDS in his work that I was aware of was David Wojnarowicz.
People were quite shocked because this wasn't what you'd see in
a New York gallery: the work was direct and it was angry. Many
artists, curators, critics, and gallerists were afraid to engage the
political dimension of the crisis. The art world was reluctant to
take on any serious discussion.

Key exceptions were Douglas Crimp, in the critical arena,
and Gran Fury, which came out of ACT UP in 1987. The New
Museum's curator Bill Olander had invited ACT UP to occupy
the window space of the New Museum that opens onto Broadway, a busy street in NYC. Bill was intent on breaking down the
distinction between art and activism. He saw the New Museum
as a valuable platform from which a political message could be
emitted. The group of interested individuals who produced the
window installation subsequently became Gran Fury.

From interview by the 12th Session of the École du Magasin. In *AIDS Riot New
York 1987–1994: Artist Collectives against AIDS*. Ed. 12th Session of the École du
Magasin, p. 289. Grenoble: Magasin, 2003.

Dan Cameron: Group Material has really retained enormous vitality as a model. Every collaborative group today is informed about what you did in some way or feels they should study and incorporate it.

Julie Ault: One of the reasons Group Material is a reference point is because it means different things to different people. That ambiguity is worth cultivating. We have not historicized ourselves or permitted our work to be historicized in one neat package. This way art students, or whoever, hear something about Group Material, start looking into it, yet never get a full picture. There are a lot of entry points into Group Material's practice, which is directly related to that fluidity in the group's process. When Group Material addresses its history, former members of the group who are interested should make it a project using the analytical and representational methods that we used originally.

Doug Ashford: Contemporary critical writing often designs too limited a trajectory for nongallery art practices. Group Material was always interested in trying to complicate definitions of both activism and art. It's really good if whoever hears about our work is inspired to redefine their practices according to their own ideas and intentions. The formal weight of political desire, its fluidity, is part of artistic process.

From "Group Material Talks to Dan Cameron," conversation with Doug Ashford and Dan Cameron. *Artforum* 41, no. 8 (April 2003): p. 253.

Judith Barry: I think you often have the chance to use exhibition design as a kind of laboratory situation. It becomes spatial thinking that cannot be performed in another way. For instance, the designs for the World's Fairs or Frederick Kiesler's *Art of the Century* or the many exhibition designs by Charles and Ray Eames or Herbert Bayer. Independent Group and Archigram are the most exemplary for me, as they overtly proposed new social and spatial paradigms. Not only did they share common objects: they were also interested in questioning the nature of what design, within the social fabric, could become. These were collaborative endeavors, and it has always made me a bit sad that their success seemed to signal their demise, even though individual authorship within both groups was maintained.

Julie Ault: I lament that there aren't more mature collaborations or more people engaged with collective production in a long-lasting way. It seems the trajectory of a lot of ideologically based collaborations is that they are temporary by design. I'm not aware of many people who embrace collaboration as a lifetime commitment in terms of practice. With rare exceptions, artistic collaboration is something people try when they are younger, and then feel that they've outgrown or should move on to develop their singular voices.

Collaboration has often been given short shrift and negatively mythologized. It is altogether omitted as a model from many schools and institutions. It is commonly believed that collaboration eclipses individual practice—when in fact they can be balanced to productively fuel one another. Being ego-oriented with a focus on individuation has been normalized. But it seems natural to be in dialogue and work with other people. The collaborative spirit gets taken out of people.

Martin Beck: One of the obstacles in that regard is that the system of valorization in the art (and culture) field works against collaboration. In order to maintain a collaborative practice in the art field you need a certain degree of idealism and also some sort of financial independence. And people do have that more frequently when they are younger—or in relation to certain social and cultural conditions, such as in the late 1960s in Italy, where for a young designer or architect to pursue an individualistic practice was seen to be complicit with a despised bourgeois ideology. So the stakes were different. Realistically, most cultural practices happen on the basis of collaboration—they are just not credited that way. So maybe it's a matter of formalizing it and publicly committing to collaborative structures as a mode of authorship.

From "Making the Politics of Display Visible," conversation with Judith Barry and Martin Beck. In Julie Ault and Martin Beck, *Critical Condition: Selected Texts in Dialogue*. Ed. Marius Babias, pp. 397–98. Essen: Kokerei Zollverein/Zeitgenössische Kunst und Kritik, 2003.

Julie Ault: Generally speaking, our practices are contextual. They are also ephemeral in that we produce temporary exhibitions and projects rather than regularly make lasting objects. I see the exhibition as a medium and as a composition that is articulated with objects and information. That articulation entails aspects of ephemeral display, including lighting, context, placement, and spacing, that create a structure and an environment.

Martin Beck: We share certain working methods. Our artistic projects—whether they are authored individually or collaboratively—do not grow out of a studio situation but develop from a research process within which themes are defined. At the same time, we investigate the particulars of a situation, of a site. That could be how a space actually looks, how it functions, what kind of discourse it puts forward, etc. These parameters become important foundations for how a project then develops.

From Julie Ault and Martin Beck, "Exhibiting X: Methods for an Open Form," lecture, Université de Lausanne, Switzerland, May 2003. In Julie Ault and Martin Beck, *Critical Condition, Selected Texts in Dialogue*. Ed. Marius Babias, p. 379. Essen: Kokerei Zollverein/Zeitgenössische Kunst und Kritik, 2003.

A fundamental issue in the ongoing debate about measuring poverty is whether poverty lines should be updated in "absolute" or "relative" fashion. Absolute measures operate with the logic that there is a calculable, nationally uniform survival level of income below which people should be considered economically deprived. The current US official measure is an absolute measure that attempts to define a basic subsistence standard and has thresholds that remain constant over time. It is updated for inflation, using the Consumer Price Index. On the other hand, relative poverty lines define poverty in terms of comparative economic disadvantage, and are assessed against relative and evolving standards of living, such as society's existing level of economic, social, and cultural development. Implicit in the relative poverty measure is the assumption that people need more than basic nutrition. Those whose resources are significantly below the resources of others, even if they are physically able to survive, may not be able to participate adequately in social organizations and in society. Relative deprivation impacts on people psychologically, physically, and materially—many people born into poverty remain in poverty.

From Julie Ault and Martin Beck, *Economies of Poverty*. Weatherspoon Museum, Greensboro, NC, 2004. Wall text for the exhibition *Borne of Necessity*.

August 2004, New York: The Kerry and Bush presidential campaigns dominated the local and national news. The Republican Convention was staged in New York City—one place in the country where there aren't any Republicans. I avoided clipping articles about either as the election media discourse did not seem to reveal much about the political underpinnings steering the period. Instead, I cut out articles about atrocious fissures in the so-called American experiment. Aggressive follies to root out difference (the supposed foundation of American society): a deadly interrogation conducted along the precipice of cultural difference, prisoners being charged room and board for their incarceration, solemn powers awarded agents at US borders, and a metaphor—botany invasion crossing the boundary into bucolic gardens. / JA

I was traveling in Europe during August—the month we were asked to cut out articles. The plan was to collect at least one newspaper or magazine from each of the cities I visited. Not speaking the languages, I was unable to read most of the texts. Instead, I tried to find correspondences between images, ads, or articles whose subjects I could only surmise. I was drawn to pictures and stories dealing with American themes or iconography but also those I could identify with in some personal way. The resulting group of clippings formed a potentially rich, though indeterminate, narrative space. / SP

From Julie Ault and Stephan Pascher, "August." *Old News* (Pork Salad Press), no. 1 (2004): p. 2.

Terms such as *freethinking* and *autonomous* are persistent characterizations of art making. While striving for independent thinking is in many ways productive and positive, in reality artistic production is both a social process and a cultural practice. Within such an open-ended framework as art school, it seems to me vitally important that the core curriculum expand its scope beyond independent work, artistic technique, and spotty art history, to focus on the investigation and analysis of the various contexts artistic production are in relation to and influenced by. These include the ideologies, histories, and current conditions of aesthetic, cultural, social, political, and economic frameworks. Correlating individuals' artistic desires with these larger contexts in a dynamic enterprise might provide, generally speaking, the means for developing critical consciousness and articulating cultural agency, which together constitute a broad agenda for contemporary art education.

From "Train of Thought: Education and Art." In *Campus. Nr. 01, Politische Mündigkeit = Political responsibility = Emancipazione politica.* Ed. Maria Eichhorn, pp. 4–5. Cologne: Walther König, 2005. Exhibition newspaper.

Corita preached meticulous ways of looking and doing. "Save everything—it might come in handy later." "Look at everything." "Pretend you are a microscope." "Make a movie with your eyes." "Look hard." "Always be around. Come or go to everything. Always go to classes. Read everything you can get your hands on. Look at movies carefully, often." "Don't blink when you're watching a movie or a cut-up page, you may miss some frames which is like missing whole pages from a book." The rules of the IHC [Immaculate Heart Community] art department also reflected Corita's philosophy. Rule four: "Consider everything an experiment." Rule six: "Nothing is a mistake. There's no win and no fail. There's only make. Anything that comes your way, including the work of artists, is a place for starting." Corita's proposal that *everything* is potentially motivating must have been tremendously refreshing, liberating students from academic traditions of what art can be and its accepted forms. The following student, after participating in a workshop with Corita, testifies:

> With our textbook ideas about art, we came together this summer, 1958, to find ourselves thrust into a whole new schema of thought. The "lights went out" in all the corridors that were thought to lead to ART and we have been left groping in what we may fear to be the wrong direction. . . .
>
> Our explorations into this new world through creative thinking, coupled with creative doing, in such projects as collages, wall books, posters, and contour drawings left us wondering (in that uncomfortable darkness!). We have been dug out of our complacent, neat little ruts and have been challenged to go beyond the narrow confines of our Puritanical heritage—to plunge—and into a whole wonderful new world of sensitive perceptions.[99]

From "The Spirited Art of Sister Corita." In *Come Alive: The Spirited Art of Sister Corita.* Ed. Julie Ault, p. 44. London: Four Corners Books, 2006.

[99.] Unattributed statement from "Summaries of Practicums," in Sister Mary Corita Kent, IHM, "Searching for the Creative Concept," *New Trends in Art Education* (Washington, DC: Catholic University of America Press, 1959).

I want to begin this book by telling you that I knew Felix Gonzalez-Torres well. I don't confide this to assert my authority, though for some it may, for others it may have a contrary effect. I do so because omission seems like hiding in view of the fact that our relationship provides the foundation for the book. Felix and I met in 1987. Quickly, we became friends and colleagues working in the collaboration Group Material. Eventually we became close friends and spent a great deal of time together until his death early in 1996. Despite my intention to impart little personal narration, Felix as I knew him is the basis from which many decisions about this volume have been reasoned. What I mean is that the cues and clues that shaped the book's concept and character come from the sum of what I know about Felix Gonzalez-Torres: the public record of his practice and art, the discourse of its circulation through exhibitions and writings, his archives, and our dialogue, which gave me insight into his thinking processes and working methods. The fact of our closeness rendered me witness to his ways of being. I cannot and do not want to discount this domain of shared experience and personal knowledge—the ephemeral realm from which this project takes form—any more than I can or want to give an account of it. Yet it is this intimate dimension with which disparate material research reconciles.

From preface to *Felix Gonzalez-Torres*. Ed. Julie Ault, p. ix. New York: Steidl Dangin, 2006.

1991   Soviet Union disintegrates into fifteen separate countries,
        thereby ending the Cold War. Its collapse is publicized by
        the West as a triumph of democracy and capitalism over
        socialism.

1992   **Jeff died of AIDS**

1992   **President Clinton—hope, twelve years of trickle-
        down economics came to an end**

1992   **the forces of hate and ignorance are alive and well
        in Oregon and Colorado, among other places**

1992   Colorado's Amendment 2, which excludes lesbians,
        gay men, and bisexuals from existing laws that prohibit
        discrimination, is approved by voters. In 1996 the US
        Supreme Court determines that the amendment is
        unconstitutional, by a vote of 6 to 3, with Justices Scalia,
        Rehnquist, and Thomas dissenting.

1992   *"Untitled,"* an image of Gonzalez-Torres's empty bed, is
        installed in twenty-four billboard spaces around the city,
        a project for the Museum of Modern Art.

1992   LA Rebellion in response to acquittal of four police
        officers who beat Rodney King.

1992   **started to collect George Nelson clocks and
        furniture**

1993   **moved to 24th Street**

1993   **Sam Nunn is such a sissy, peace might be possible
        in the Middle East**

1993   **three years since Ross died, painted kitchen floor
        bright orange, this book** (New York: A.R.T. Press,
        1993).

1993   Final stack piece, *"Untitled" (Passport #II)*, composed of
        pamphlets with images of sky, clouds, and birds.

1993   Gonzalez-Torres finishes *"Untitled" (Portrait of Ingvild
        Goetz)*, which, he says, "embodies a very clear system of
        what constitutes a 'portrait.'"

1993   Gonzalez-Torres produces *"Untitled" (Placebo—Landscape
        —for Roni)*, gold-wrapped candies, last of the candy pieces.

1994   Canada, the United States, and Mexico launch the North
        American Free Trade Agreement (NAFTA) and form the
        world's largest free-trade area.

1994   *Traveling*, an exhibition of Gonzalez-Torres at the Museum
        of Contemporary Art, Los Angeles; the Hirshhorn
        Museum and Sculpture Garden, Washington, DC; and
        the Renaissance Society at the University of Chicago.

1994   *"Untitled" (America)* is the last of twenty-four light-
        string pieces made over two years, which Gonzalez-
        Torres calls "my own history of light."

1995   Retrospective exhibition of Gonzalez-Torres at the
        Solomon R. Guggenheim Museum, New York.

1995   Gonzalez-Torres makes his last version of his self-portrait
        for exhibition at the Centro Galego de Arte Contempora-
        neo, Santiago de Compostela, Spain. Text reads:
        *Red Canoe 1987 Watercolors 1964 Paris 1985 Supreme
        Court 1986 Blue Lake 1986 Our Own Apartment 1976
        Rosa 1977 Güaimaro 1957 New York City 1979 Pebbles
        and Biko 1985 Ross 1983 Civil Rights Act 1964 Mariel
        Boatlift 1980 White Shirt 1984 Julie 1987 An Easy
        Death 1991 CNN 1980 Black Monday 1987 Berlin Wall
        1989 Great Society 1964 Venice 1985 Wawanaisa Lake
        1987 U.N. 1945 Mother 1986 Myriam 1990 VCR 1978
        Dad 1991 Bay of Pigs 1961 D-Day 1944 Interferon 1989*

*Jeff 1978 Silver Ocean 1990 H-Bomb 1954 The World I
Knew Is Gone 1991 Bruno and Mary 1991 Madrid 1971
MTV 1981 Rafael 1992 May 1968 Andrea 1990 Twenty-
fourth Street 1993 LA 1990 Placebo 1991 George Nelson
Clocks 1993 A view to remember 1995.*

From Julie Ault and Felix Gonzalez-Torres (posthumously), "Chronology." In *Felix Gonzalez-Torres*. Ed. Julie Ault, pp. 373–75. New York: Steidl Dangin, 2006.

* Entries in bold constitute the biogra-
phy Felix Gonzalez-Torres wrote for
Felix Gonzalez-Torres (New York:
A.R.T. Press, 1993).

Tillmans creates exhibitory contexts with his photographs. Actively engaging in these situations interrupts the imposture of objectivity and disrupts the codes by which many art institutions disseminate art to publics. Tillmans's belief in his own complex, flexible subjectivity—and the extension of its validity to one and all—inspire his methods, which subtly decenter institutional installation authority and redistribute display.

Identity is irresolute. Self-construction, deconstruction, and reconstruction are vital dimensions of Tillmans's artistic formation. His practice reflects continually shifting subjectivity, necessitating that design always be new. The artist's conviction that identity is flexile and unclassifiable, and his concomitant repertoire of display stratagems, make it possible to sustain an active relationship to his history—through his images—and to presentational formations that mediate meaning.

From "The Subject Is Exhibition." In *Wolfgang Tillmans*, pp. 121–26. New Haven: Yale University Press, 2006. Exhibition catalogue.

Martin Beck: We understand and have understood cultural or artistic authorship not as something that is confined to a single medium or a limited set of practices but as something that is at the core of art and cultural practice; and as such it is something that is continuously contested. We decided to bypass limitations of what an author can be in the framework of an exhibition, wanting to explode the concept of what artistic authorship can offer in the thinking through of the show. We did this not as a ploy but as something that we increasingly became aware of in trying to understand our own methodologies in relation to this exhibition, as well as in relation to our practices. We became interested in seeing, in making visible, in the format of an exhibition, what the scope of that kind of practice can be.

Julie Ault: The exhibition is structured by a set of arenas that are individually authored, in the case of *Rumor* by Martin, or the *Corita* arena, organized by myself, and then the *Information* project and the *Dialogue* video, which are collaborations between us, as well as other parts. And to keep in mind the exhibition as a whole as our primary medium; the exhibition as a communication form in itself.

Let's start talking about our initial understanding of the space and how we worked with it. When we were invited to do an exhibition at the Secession a couple of years ago, Martin had more familiarity, obviously, with this kind of space. But I, coming from the US, and not having done many exhibitions in large exhibition halls in Europe, was somewhat intimidated by the architectural features and the history of the Secession as the quintessential white-cube prototype. Martin and I talked a lot about how to work with this space and decided not to make an architectural intervention, decorate it, or do anything that embellishes the space but instead to take the spatial structure "as is," to highlight the gallery's status as both historical artifact and present-day policy. One of the issues we continuously consider is how do you engage with what you put into a space.

What are the display tactics? The presentational mode? We wanted to engage the space as it is. The only treatment we have applied to the permanent structure is to install a series of photographs by artist Felix Gonzalez-Torres on the exterior walls of the gallery. Within this frame, everything we wanted to show was built from the ground up. Each element is organized and designed in order to accommodate a very specific set of materials. The fixtures are freestanding and mostly ephemeral in order to disappear after the show ends.

From Julie Ault and Martin Beck, gallery talk, Secession, Vienna, September 2006. In *The Secession Talks: Exhibitions in Conversation 1998–2010*. Ed. Sylvia Liska, pp. 483–84. Cologne: Walther König, 2012.

Julie Ault: In its first incarnation, Printed Matter had a community feel inside it as well as a community-building function, which changed to some degree with the move from Lispenard to Wooster Street. Printed Matter in essence functions as a store but has always been simultaneously a distribution site that essentially exhibits what is for sale, mounts exhibitions within its space, holds events, etc. That hybrid aspect of being part store, part nonprofit venue presents some perceptual problems, particularly in terms of funding. I recall when I was on the board in the 1990s being dismayed by the organization's perpetual insolvency. In order to compete in the contemporary field, which clearly has changed dramatically since the early 1980s, Printed Matter became more commercial in the sense that the offerings are not exclusively artist's books and there is greater attention to selling so as to operate in the black along current lines of thinking. How has that shift come across to you?

Lucy R. Lippard: Printed Matter was originally a community of radical/avant-garde/experimental (not always the same thing) artists. We were the only place artist's-book makers could go, and we always got flack when anything was rejected from the store. Whoever was running it at the time did the choosing, and maybe the board got involved when controversy arose. Printed Matter was an incredible support system for artists (despite its insolvency and various organizational problems). I lost interest to some extent when it became mostly a commercial endeavor. But it couldn't succeed without doing that. It's the story of so many nonprofits. . . . With my resounding lack of talent for structure and finance, I can't throw the first stone.

From "Interview with Lucy R. Lippard on Printed Matter." Printed Matter, December 2006. https://printedmatter.org/tables/41.

Clearly, artistic production as social process and collaboration should not be essentialized or regarded as mandatory, to be taught according to formulas laid out in curriculum reports. That kind of regimentation is antithetical to the principles of dynamic collaborative process and would certainly undermine its discursive character, which is so valuable as method for thinking and acting. In this mix, which is in part a discussion of institutionalization, there is a risk of rendering social engagement and collaboration into genres and medias as opposed to ways of working, guiding principles, or operating systems. But from our perspectives, the values of collaboration and collectivity—their inherent tendency to complexify and contextualize—need to be amply represented, theorized, and experienced in the context of art education. In art education, collaborative structures and process *as a mode of authorship* need to be effectively brought into the field of models that are referenced, articulated, and investigated, including through practice.

From Julie Ault and Martin Beck, "Drawing Out & Leading Forth." In *Notes for an Art School*. Ed. Mai Abu ElDahab, Anton Vidokle, and Florian Waldvogel, pp. 44–45. Nicosia: Manifesta 6 School Books, 2006.

Data issued by the Congressional Budget Office (CBO) shows that "the income gap in 2000 was the widest it has been since 1979, and likely was the widest it has been in 70 years. . . . Income was more concentrated at the very top of the income spectrum in 2002 . . . than in all but six years since the mid-1930s. . . . Further, some of the tax cuts that were enacted in 2001 are still being phased in. . . . Those at the top of the income scale continue to receive an exceptionally large share of the nation's income."

Although circumstances in the private economy principally influence income disparities, government policy can certainly encourage or mitigate the growing disproportion. David Francis, reporting for the *Christian Science Monitor* on May 23, 2001, stated, "President Bush's tax cut promises to have a side effect that bothers many Americans: widening the gap between rich and poor. . . . But Bush and congressional Republicans rest the tax cut on their own argument of fairness: It is the prosperous who pay the bulk of income taxes, so they should get most of the tax relief." Tax experts generally agree that the Bush tax cuts enacted since 2001 widen income disparities further than ever before in US history.

From Julie Ault and Martin Beck, "Tracing the Bush Tax Cuts." In *Installation*. New York: Storefront for Art and Architecture; Vienna: Secession, 2006. Exhibition handout.

This is a diary of a conversation. Diaries are self-conscious by nature.

Cross-references composed of speculations, asides, questions, reflections, anecdotes, suggestions, etc. Have you seen *Still Water*? Have you read *Another Water*? Speaking about *Still Water*, Roni said, *The image is one part of the form, the viewer is the second, and the voice in the footnotes is the third. This voice is mainly characterized by an endless flow of consciousness. In parts of the text it anticipates the viewer. It is also my voice. I am there with you as you look at these images. I'm talking to you.*[8]

Water and Roni Horn, open-ended.

There's nothing extraneous in Roni Horn. I want to follow suit.

I am a wayfaring commentator drifting around Roni Horn. Can something be roundabout that has no destination?

I'm dittoing a method to experience the freedom her practice motions toward. How could I not think about form anew when engaged in Roni Horn's work?

Roni's new project, *VATNASAFN / LIBRARY OF WATER* is "open, to anyone, at the time of their choosing, on their own, or with others."[9]

I would love for all the viewers of Roni Horn's work to gather and form a crowd—a motley bunch I suspect.

I use her first and last name over and over because together they are complete.

From "Faith Is Doubt Is Roni Horn." In *Roni Horn*, pp. 9–10. Seoul: Kukje Gallery, 2007. Exhibition catalogue.

[8] Roni Horn, "Lynne Cooke in Conversation with Roni Horn," in *Roni Horn* (London: Phaidon, 2000), p. 20.

[9] See www.libraryofwater.is.

Benning's work is as much a record of his consciousness in time and place, and therefore memory and how he incorporates time and place within himself, as it is concerned with society, industry, race, history, landscape, the Midwest, the American West, and America at large.

The methodological centrality of the personal carries through his complete oeuvre. He has commented: "It's not hard for me to tell things about myself personally—that's the easy part. The hard part about making personal work is not to make it one man's problem—not to make a film that just refers to my own grief. Who cares about that? I want people to be able to enter the film through their own lives. . . . But by myself being open I think they can be open to themselves. That's what I think a personal film has to do—has to show a trust but then it has to become more meaningful than what that story is about. It has to be bigger."[64]

Benning's films invite us to enter into dialogue with the world through private narrative, journey, intimacy, and solitude. An undertow of personal rumination and transformation is exposed in order to open outward and link to larger collective forces. We learn from his art that the personal is not a discrete realm: it is a far-reaching and empowering connective force that describes and inscribes the individual and the world simultaneously.

From "Using the Earth as a Map of Himself: The Personal Conceptualism of James Benning." In *James Benning*. Ed. Barbara Pichler and Claudia Slanar, pp. 111–12. Vienna: Filmmuseum Vienna, 2007.

[64] James Benning, in Reinhard Wulf, *James Benning: Circling the Image* (Westdeutscher Rundfunk [WDR], Germany, 2003), film.

The War on Poverty did not call for redistribution of wealth to redress the "paradox of poverty in the midst of plenty." Historian James T. Patterson has written, "The poverty program, like other government efforts of the early 1960s, reflected a conservative application of structuralist observations. The planners recognized that millions of the so-called new poor were not in the labor force, that they need income maintenance more than opportunity. They knew that formidable structural forces like technological change, shortages of decent paying jobs and racial discrimination blocked the opportunities of many who were willing and able to work." As [Michael] Harrington put it, "There never was a massive investment of billions of dollars in radical innovations that challenged the very structure of power in the United States." The power structure of American capitalism and its accompanying socioeconomic stratification remained intact, as they continue today.

From Julie Ault and Martin Beck, "Tracing the War on Poverty." *Art Lies*, no. 56 (Winter 2007): p. 45.

Americana included work by overtly socially engaged artists, many of whom were women and artists of color, and popular "commercial artists" as well as store-bought objects from so-called low culture. In terms of the look of the show, it was designed to be dense and layered, viewed first as a whole (as democratic) rather than as discrete (autonomous) objects. We purchased many rolls of contact paper, the inexpensive decorative self-adhesive wallpaper, in diverse patterns, mostly coded as "American." Strips of the patterned paper were laid like stripes from floor to ceiling, forming a ground of diverse designs upon which objects were hung. Over fifty artists' works were selected for inclusion, as well as products from supermarkets and department stores. Store-bought items, such as a selection of laundry detergents, were installed in groupings that—with a degree of irony—demonstrated "freedom of choice." A television was hooked up, which broadcast whatever was on major network programming continuously. A washing machine and dryer dominated center stage as the only other sculptural elements. A sound track made up of songs "representative of America" sampled from various genres was on continuous play. The total effect of *Americana* was overstimulating with no space in the room left "neutral." In *Americana*, space was densely instrumentalized distinct from the rest of the biennial, which, except for a couple installations, was installed on the standard sixty-inch hanging line.

One organizing goal was to schematize and make material some problematic divisions and hierarchies within the art and culture industry. The boundaries between "high" and "low" culture were symbolically dislodged in *Americana*.

From "Three Snapshots from the Eighties." In *Curating Subjects*. Ed. Paul O'Neill, p. 35. London: Open Editions, 2007.

For Tillmans, the exhibition space is an arena: a threshold is crossed upon entering. Exhibition rooms are treated entirely, articulated by photographs with attention to their pictorial and sculptural dimensions and their relations to the architecture. Spatial intervals are vital and can vary to help generate anything from "salon-style" hangings to discrete and linear installations and a wide range of hybrids. Tillmans decides on manner or combination of modes from discerning what he deems best for the work within each particular context and architectural setting. The effect may be spectacular, but rather than becoming a spectacle the result is subtle, inviting perception over reverence. The artist's installations bid us to maneuver physically, visually, and mentally, and to derive illumination and pleasure as active visitors keenly addressed. The capacity to engage, experience, and relate to his photographs—and the spaces that they open in and around them—is galvanized. By presenting some photographs unglazed, simply as paper in all its vulnerability, they also function as minimal sculptural elements. This ephemeral, sculptural quality of Tillmans's installations contributes to their effective, intimate atmosphere of trust and respect.

From "The Subject Is Exhibition (2008): Installation as Possibility in the Practice of Wolfgang Tillmans." In *Wolfgang Tillmans: Lighter*. Ed. Joachim Jäger, p. 17. Berlin: Hatje Cantz, 2008.

He was going on and on about which title to use. I suggested he
let my mother decide, she is profoundly psychic. "That's a great
idea." I called her a few days later: "A friend of mine is working
on an exhibition. His name is Danh Vo. He's contemplating two
titles and can't decide which one to use." Without inflection,
I told her the alternatives. She used a pendulum to pick up the
energy of each, checked again to be certain, and said emphati-
cally, "'Where the lions are' is the strongest." I posed another
question: "He's trying to obtain a couple of old chandeliers from
the Hotel Majestic in Paris for the show; do you think he'll succeed?" Pause. "It's more yes than no, but not a sure thing. He
has a pretty good chance though; he seems extremely focused."
A minute passed . . . "I think he'll be able to get them."

A few weeks later, in Buenos Aires, our dialogue intensified.
We went there with that in mind. We also had in mind that
I would write an essay for his publication in order to manifest
thought lines, fragments, and reference points of our exchange.
New points of contact came forward. Certain authors and writings that I had been reading lately resounded in relation to his
work. The period was exuberant and exhausting; we thrived on
and suffered from utter mental saturation. After the trip, I
selected and linked together five texts in order to mirror his
thinking, sensibility, methods, and outlook through diverse
voices. I gave the sequence a title, "Death Sentence," by Julie
Ault, for Danh Vo, and for *Where the Lions Are*.

From *Hic Svnt Leones*. Ed. Julie Ault and Danh Vo, p. 54. Basel: Kunsthalle Basel,
2009. Exhibition catalogue.

Five years later, after I resigned from NASA, we made our first trip
to Cape Kennedy. A few military units still guarded the derelict
gantries, but already the former launching site was being used as a
satellite graveyard. As the dead capsules lost orbital velocity, they
homed onto the master radio beacon. As well as the American
vehicles, Russian and French satellites in the joint Euro-American
space projects were brought down here, the burned-out hulks of
the capsules exploding across the cracked concrete.

Already, too, the relic hunters were at Cape Kennedy, scour-
ing the burning saw grass for instrument panels and flying suits
and—most valuable of all—the mummified corpses of the
dead astronauts.

These blackened fragments of collarbone and shin, kneecap
and rib, were the unique relics of the Space Age, as treasured as
the saintly bones of mediaeval shrines. After the first fatal acci-
dent in space, public outcry demanded that these orbiting biers
be brought down to Earth. Unfortunately, when a returning
moon rocket crashed into the Kalahari Desert, aboriginal tribes-
men broke into the vehicle. Believing the crew to be dead gods,
they cut off the eight hands and vanished into the bush. It had
taken two years to track them down. From then on, the capsules
were left in orbit to burn out on re-entry.

Whatever remains survived the crash landings in the satellite
graveyard were scavenged by the relic hunters of Cape Kennedy.
This band of nomads had lived for years in the wrecked cars and
motels, stealing their icons under the feet of the wardens who
patrolled the concrete decks. In early October, when a former NASA
colleague told me that Robert Hamilton's satellite was becoming
unstable, I drove down to Tampa and began to inquire about the
purchase price of Robert's mortal remains. Five thousand dollars
was a small price to pay for laying his ghost to rest in Judith's mind.

From "Death Sentence." In *Hic Svnt Leones*. Ed. Julie Ault and Danh Vo, p. 37.
Basel: Kunsthalle Basel, 2009. Exhibition catalogue. Reprint of J. G. Ballard, "The
Dead Astronaut." In *Memories of the Space Age*, pp. 67–78. Sauk City, WI: Arkham
House Publishers, 1988.

Tim

SEPTEMBER 1973. This is how I remember it: It was the first day of school at University of Maine at Augusta. Petrified, I entered the prefab art department building, on the edge of campus. There he was, with pale, translucent skin, piercing dark eyes, and shoulder-length black hair. He wore black-and-white polka-dot platform shoes, jeans, a white shirt, and a black suit coat adorned with glittering thrift-store pins. And he was coming my way, a big bag of candy in his hand. "Would you like a Tootsie Pop?" *Would I?* Tootsie Pops were my favorite, and he had all the flavors. I reached in and chose several. He later confided the candy was a strategy to smooth the way for making friends, which had been difficult for him in high school. It certainly worked in my case: I was smitten. Tim was eighteen, and I was fifteen. I had left high school after only two years, under the pretext of studying art, an option not offered at Winthrop High. He took me under his wing, and our lifelong friendship began.

MAY 1974. Tim steered me into the art-department library, which I had never visited. We sat at a round table looking at the volumes he selected—Gregory Battcock's *The New Art*, Lucy Lippard's *Six Years*. They seemed intriguing enough, but required that I read, which was something I didn't much do. Then he showed me *the book*, the one that inspired him so and changed his life—Germano Celant's *Arte Povera*. I didn't really understand what I saw, but the force of Tim's enthusiasm made me try. In my memory's eye the book consists solely of grainy black-and-white photos that cover the pages edge to edge. One image in particular rocked my world: a line drawn underwater with an electric current—was it neon? I could not fathom how that worked, but found it thrilling and poetic. Tim had opened the door to a larger world than I knew existed.

1973–1975. Tim was an overachiever (still is), relentlessly curious and critical, well read, confident, articulate, and fearless. His knowledge of contemporary art and theory surpassed that of our teachers. He became the star student of the department, his every move attracting school-wide attention and debate. He got a woman who looked like his mother to iron clothes in front of an audience for hours as part of his performance series about his family's working-class conditions. He and another student, my cousin George, stole some dirt from the yard of the governor's mansion one night and sent him a ransom note demanding he pay $10,000 for its safe return. To fulfill a sculpture assignment, he wrapped metal bands around a set of trees, creating a horizontal plane in the woods behind the art building and provoking an ad hoc protest from a couple [of] students who worried he was harming the trees. For a self-portrait assignment, he meticulously rendered his eyes but obscured the lower part of his face with a bandit-style bandana. Tim once mounted posters of suggestive images around campus advertising a flick called *Blue Movie*, and then screened a brief Super 8 monochromatic film showing a completely blue screen. That conceptual trick really pissed off the jocks who had lined up outside the auditorium in rowdy anticipation of a porno movie and booed during the screening. It was exhilarating and frightening. Tim, always courting interaction, was elated.

Back then I was an underachiever, working at Sampson's supermarket as a cashier and taking classes in Augusta to escape my hometown of Winthrop, where I had turned to hanging out with an older crowd of mostly male hippie bikers. I didn't read anything other than *Cosmopolitan* and felt profoundly insecure. I had lucked into the program at the university and, more important, the group of friends who cohered there. I had no idea, however, what kind of art I wanted to make, although for over a year I saved every cash-register receipt from my shifts at the supermarket, in hopes of eventually "doing something with them." I struggled with the assignments. Yet through all my tentative and unformed efforts, Tim acted as though everything I did showed seeds of brilliance. My first dose of wholehearted encouragement! Tim had a gift for recognizing a creative glimmer in others before they felt it themselves.

JUNE 1975. We finished the program. Tim had a plan: he would get accepted to School of Visual Arts (SVA), to study with Joseph Kosuth, procure scholarships and loans, move to New York, and become a practicing, and eventually famous, artist—which is what he did. I had no plan—no desire, money, or support to continue school, only a resolute aim to leave Maine and move to a city in another state.

FALL 1975. Tim was cut out for New York. Ever curious and ravenous for culture, he absorbed all the city could offer. He had done his research and went directly to the legendary places of contemporary art. He even rented a room in the Chelsea Hotel for a period, despite it taking so much of his budget. He was determined to live his vision and he seemed to relish every minute of it. He flourished at SVA and soon began working for Kosuth as well as in the school library. He attended every exhibition, performance, panel, and event he could. Tim's letters enthusiastically detailed his diverse experiences and all that he was seeing. One day I received a package containing documentation of a piece he had made called *Student Work*. A transparent plastic envelope held a time card indicating the hours Tim punched in for courses, student activities, and studio time at SVA in a given period. He annotated inconsistencies on the card, for instance when the punch clock malfunctioned, forcing him to register the time by hand. The oaktag time card in its clear plastic sleeve is wrapped in tracing paper, which is signed, titled, stamped, and dated, and carries an explanation of all the piece's content as well. Tim's mother, Charlotte, had said, "New York is for mutants," and we definitely fit the bill, at least in the environment of rural Maine. I realized New York was inevitable, but initially chose Washington, DC, home of Yolanda Hawkins, a friend and fellow student at Augusta, where I worked at a dry cleaners by day, in a take-out joint by night, as an occasional usher at the Kennedy Center, and pursued little else.

SEPTEMBER 1976. Tim found a big, cheap apartment for us, and I moved to Manhattan, along with Yolanda. I worked at Baskin Robbins (my all-time-favorite job) and then as a telephone operator. My artistic, cultural, social, and political education continued thanks to Tim and his new friends, assisted by New York City.

Tim frequently brought cultural work to my attention. We shared and savored the music of James Brown, Betty Wright, Rufus and Chaka Khan, Esther Phillips, Labelle, Steve Reich, Frederic Rzewski, Martha Reeves, and X-Ray Spex; the art of Alexander Rodchenko, Jannis Kounellis, Nancy Spero, and Odilon Redon; the poems of Vladimir Mayakovsky; the designs of Enzo Mari; the writings of Wilhelm Reich and Lucy Lippard; the films of George Romero and Pier Paolo Pasolini; and much more.

OCTOBER 1978. We were on a plane; I don't recall where we were headed. Tim was looking at an art catalogue and critiquing: "Oh my god, look at that!" Then, "This one's not so great." I asked him how he knew some artworks were good and some not. He lit up at the opportunity. "Well, let's take a look." We went through the catalogue page by page. He didn't say a word, and asked me to tell him what I thought. Silence. I was tongue-tied. He waited. "Go on, just take a look and say what you think." More silence. I was so nervous. "What about this one here?" I took a chance. "Well, I like it but I don't know why." Tim was expressionless. I went on, "This one doesn't do anything for me," "This seems kind of great," and so on. Tim was soon smiling. "See, you *do* know what works and what doesn't." So our opinions were in sync, but only after this demonstration did he steer the conversation toward what factors codetermine the processes of evaluating art, and what problems emerge within those dynamics. Always teaching.

FALL 1979. We were talking in the kitchen after work, and Tim announced everyone was ready to start the collaborative group we had long imagined assembling and begin to work together. "Everyone" meant Patrick Brennan, his fellow student and friend from NYU—as well as Marybeth Nelson, Beth Jaker, Peter Szypula, and Hannah Alderfer, his close friends from Kosuth's class, who had also become my friends. We identified some other possible participants, including Yolanda Hawkins and Marek Pakulski, the bass player for the Fleshtones. I remember feeling excited about formalizing a group from this circle, while not really knowing what it might accomplish or become. That enterprise became Group Material, to which I belonged for seventeen years. Although we all created it, and those who joined later helped develop it as well, Tim proved a primary force in Group Material until he left late in 1987 to focus on his work with K.O.S.

Tim is a born teacher, and I became his earliest unofficial student. He understands what it means to feel underdeveloped and yearning, and he fashions methods to counter those conditions. His buoyant attention draws forth latent capacities. He propels people to grow and to learn how to trust themselves. He nourishes by example. He catalyzes. He prods. He cajoles. And he continually signposts potential paths for discovery, action, and agency.

For Tim, art inherently involves teaching and learning, the symbiotic passions at the core of his being. For Tim, art is a social practice—a collaboration with history and with people in the present. His disposition—already apparent at eighteen— comes across thirty-five years later through the testament of practice: in bodies of work produced collaboratively, in the

group structures he has catalyzed, and in the individuals transformed by their connection with Tim, forever changed by their
joint actions.

From *Tim Rollins and K.O.S.: A History*. Ed. Ian Berry, pp. 13–14. Cambridge, MA:
MIT Press; Saratoga Springs, NY: Frances Young Tang Teaching Museum and
Art Gallery, Skidmore College, 2009.

It isn't so much their relationship on the line as his worldview at stake.

(Oh, that sinking feeling of waking up the morning after taking in bad news—of betrayal, disgrace, or a loved one's death. It takes a few seconds to orient consciousness, and then, bam—the shattering force of revelation. Heartsick, grief, despair. In time, inevitably, we settle down. Acceptance and resolve set in, but the undercurrent is devastating.)

She pours his coffee. Routine gestures. Speechless intimacy. Uneasy harmony. Anxious affection. Domesticity. Comfort. Pact. Habit. No rocking boat here. They have minimal contact, negligible engagement. Safe. Muted.

> The contract was like an emotional spell cast over the relationship at the beginning to exempt her from contingency, to pre-empt the inevitable uncertainties of evolving time. (Adam Phillips, *On Flirtation*, page 7)

> There we are, hoping that the flimsy social safety nets we've committed ourselves to—monogamy, domesticity, maturity—resolve our anxieties; that "security" or "commitment" (or children, or real estate) are functional salves, even if the fetid quantities of apprehension pooled just beneath the floorboards bode a different story. (Laura Kipnis, *Against Love*, page 57f)

Is this simply a typical morning spent protecting one another's solitude, or are they both beset with confusion, resignation, and fear? Too many emotions tumbling around to put into words. Immersed in couple grammar, the aesthetics of their relationship demonstrate the complications.

From "A word that has the power to change one's life." In *Everness*. Ed. Alejandro Cesarco, pp. 9–10. New York: Murray Guy, 2009. Exhibition brochure.

In 2004, while leafing through Lucy Lippard's legendary volume *Six Years: The Dematerialization of the Art Object from 1966 to 1972*, I paused with fresh interest on the photograph of a man doing a handstand atop a rocky peak in a big-skied landscape. His straight graceful form appears effortless, despite being inches away from a substantial plunge. The image filled me with exhilarating tension and elicited contradictory impressions of gravity and airiness, serenity and adventure, and audacity and fright.[1]

The man on the mountaintop is California-based artist Robert Kinmont (b. 1937). The paradoxical photograph is the first of the series *8 Natural Handstands* (1969) and is an arresting document of a sculptural act embodying discipline, verve, self-assurance, and transcendence, all of which, I would learn, are characteristics of the artist himself. Lippard's book briefly mentions another work, *My Favorite Dirt Roads*, which I immediately conjured up since there was no illustration.

My interest was kindled—I wanted to know more about Robert Kinmont; however, information was sparse, and he had disappeared from public circulation more than twenty-five years earlier. As my anticipation grew I projected a mythic nature onto the elusive artist. Four years passed before, in an old-fashioned classroom–*cum*–community center in Sonoma, I met the reclusive Kinmont and finally saw much of the diversely formed, distinctive art he made between 1958 and the mid-1970s, as well as recent works. I was thrilled to have my high expectations simultaneously met and brought down to earth.

From *In Step with the Desert: The Morphology of Robert Kinmont*, n.p. New York: Alexander and Bonin, 2009. Exhibition catalogue.

[1.] Lucy R. Lippard, *Six Years: The Dematerialization of the Art Object from 1966 to 1972* (New York: Praeger, 1973), pp. 69–70. At that time, Martin Beck and I were curating an exhibition, *Mirage*, to take place at Alexander and Bonin in the summer of 2005, which would include Kinmont's work.

Spero's decision, made in 1974, that women would be the subjects of all her future works was a natural outgrowth of her feminist activities. "I decided to view women and men by representing women," she said, "not just to reverse history, but to see what it means to view the world through the depiction of women." Drawing on an Amnesty International report, she created *Torture of Women* (1974–76), a 125-foot-long piece composed of collaged elements including painted cutout female figures, severed heads, mythological monsters, goddesses, and excerpts from the ancient Sumerian myth of Tiamat's brutal dismemberment by Marduk; all this shares space with eyewitness accounts of state-sanctioned torture, written on a bulletin typewriter or printed via letterpress. These stories of women being battered, burned, cut, electrocuted, raped, split open, and murdered are wrenching to read, their sheer geographic and historical reach shocking.

Around this time, a chance remark by the proprietor of a printshop inspired Spero to begin transferring her painted figures to zinc plates, which permitted her to reproduce, repeat, and recycle images freely and infinitely; previously, she had always painted her figures by hand. In the ensuing years, she frequently spoke of "cannibalizing" her work, a methodological by-product of the printing technique she adopted. "I was like a director of a stock company and these characters would appear, disappear, and reappear . . ."

From "Voice Recognition: Julie Ault on Nancy Spero." *Artforum* 48, no. 6 (February 2010): p. 54.

Institutions get on the industry treadmill just as individuals do. It's no secret that the art industry collectively suffers from a cultivated form of attention deficit disorder. Art institutions likewise appear unwilling and unable to entertain ambiguity or include periods for behind-the-scenes reflection and exploration geared toward deepening their work and their methods. Were cultural institutions to regard their process as a creative one that is reflexive, doubt ridden, and productively discontinuous rather than a bureaucratic one that rigidly and arrogantly takes itself and its ways for granted, some benefits might ensue. The notion of the time-out—time to analyze, to think, to inquire and reflect—is essential to any dynamic enterprise. Perhaps the most important questions any institution, organization, or individual practitioner can periodically pose inward (as well as publicly) are, "Why do this? Is there need? Is there desire? Does my/our work fill a void? What is at stake beyond immediate pressures and deadlines? What would happen if we stopped and took stock? What if we closed our doors for a month? A year? Could it be productive? How would we do things differently if we didn't do what we're doing, if we threw the manual out the window? *Why is today the same as every other day?*"

From "Of Several Minds over Time." In *Playing by the Rules: Alternative Thinking | Alternative Spaces*. Ed. Steven Rand, pp. 102–3. New York: Apexart, 2010.

I look for the exit and pass through the galleries again on my way out. I overhear a disgruntled viewer: "They didn't even give her an audio tour." (Ah, a venue for my inner reflections.) I began composing on the spot:

Highlights and focal points are irrelevant in Roni Horn aka Roni Horn. *Nothing is superfluous. Everything you see here has been explicitly chosen by the artist. Look at every work, freely and carefully. Don't miss a moment. Don't miss an inch. Don't miss a trick. This is the only time you'll see these works together in this configuration in these spaces, installed by the artist with such precision. Experience Roni Horn's work here and now. You don't need to know more than what you see. It's all here.* (Insert artist's voice: "You walk into the room unquestioning. You take responsibility for being there. In the end I am not interested in what the viewer knows about my intention or identity. I am trying to make the meaning of the work and one's experience of it the same.")[13] *Take your time. Move through the show from one direction and double back through and see it all again in reverse. Look closely and then from a distance. Change your position. Walk around the work. Be in the work. There is no ideal perspective. Look from one room into the next to where other works beckon. Relish the sightlines. Turn around and see where you came from. Watch others looking. Eavesdrop. See how the works clarify one another. Absorb the buildup of experience. Books, drawings, sculptures, photographs, installations. Notice the interplay of media, material, subject matter, colors, and methods across the works, and between the fresh memories of the show you experience as you move through it along with your experience right now.* (Insert artist's voice: "I don't see the media or idioms as isolated and there are no hierarchies among them, so I shift

13. Louise Neri, "Roni Horn: To Fold,"
in *Roni Horn* (London: Phaidon,
2000), p. 53.

between them freely . . .")[14] *Free your experience from expectations. Linger in the culture of Roni Horn. Be here now. Start over. Stay longer than you planned. Have fun.* (Insert artist's voice: "I have this ambition to make the meaning of a work people's experience of it. Every eyewitness is an authority.")[15] *Realize Roni Horn.*

From "What a Pair: Roni Horn aka Roni Horn." In *Roni Horn: Well and Truly.* Ed. Yilmaz Dziewior, pp. 50–51. Bregenz: Kunsthaus Bregenz, 2010. Exhibition catalogue.

[14] Matthew Barney et al., *Roni Horn aka Roni Horn*, vol. 2, *Subject Index* (London: Tate Modern; Göttingen: Steidl Verlag, 2009), p. 49.

[15] Ibid., p. 12.

The inaugural exhibition includes a window installation of montages made by Peter, Marybeth, Hannah, and Beth, an installation by Conrad Atkinson, works by Michael Lebron, Klaus Staeck, and other group members. Lili's piece, *Budgets*, consists of ten papers pinned to a bulletin board. Although they are not identified by name, they reflect the budgets of Group Material members. A calendar of upcoming exhibitions and information about the group is distributed. The night before the show opens, Tim is setting up his piece, which includes stenciling text in red paint on the floor, while a stereo with Martha and the Vandellas' "Dancing in the Street," also a part of his work, is on continuous play. It is unclear if the paint will dry in time and whether or not the show will be ready for the reception. As the Vandellas' song plays repeatedly, tensions mount, and everyone begins yelling at one another.

From "Chronicle: 1979–1996." In *Show and Tell: A Chronicle of Group Material*. Ed. Julie Ault, p. 18. London: Four Corners Books, 2010.

Group Material should not be reduced to memory or record but can most constructively be articulated and elaborated by the dynamics between multiple bodies of information. Somewhere between the representation of lived experience of events and their contexts and the nonjudgmental multiplicity of the archive, historical representation gets complex and exciting. The history of history is fraught with what Derrida calls "an incessant tension between the archive and archaeology." He continues, "They will always be close the one to the other, resembling each other, hardly discernible in their coimplication, and yet radically incompatible, heterogeneous . . ."[7] Perhaps imprint and memory are not mutually hostile, and the conflict between archive and memory is overestimated. What if we understand History and Memory as inseparable, accept their apparent coproductive roles, and refuse to regard this as a predicament?

From "Case Reopened: Group Material." In *Show and Tell: A Chronicle of Group Material*. Ed. Julie Ault, p. 216. London: Four Corners Books, 2010.

[7] Jacques Derrida, *Archive Fever: A Freudian Impression*, trans. Eric Prenowitz (Chicago: University of Chicago Press, 1995), p. 92.

While retrieving Group Material for myself, for the group, and with the larger purpose of public representation in mind, inhabiting the dual roles of observer and observed created a central methodological challenge, which at times was confounding. Flipping between my own and other members' muddle of memory as well as the accumulation of material sometimes felt like too much and not enough. But, ultimately my insider relationship to the subject in conjunction with a more independent association to the potential for archives to shape historical representation seemed to productively balance one another.

From "Historical Inquiry as Subject and Object." *Índex*, no. 0 (Autumn 2010): p. 24.

Ballard conjures the massive transformation of social order and form engendered by technological and media environments in eroticized car crashes that mark the symbolic elegance of the highway system ("a huge reticular prison, granting the illusion of speed, direction and self-chosen destiny");[1] in the spatial pockets of no-man's-land—traffic islands produced by auto circulation; and in the idealized order of the high-rise as a dynamic force in which "a new social type was being created . . . a cool, unemotional personality impervious to the psychological pressure of high-rise life, with minimal needs for privacy, who thrived like an advanced species of machine in the neutral atmosphere . . . the sort of resident content to do nothing but sit in his overpriced apartment, watch television with the sound turned down, and wait for his neighbors to make a mistake."[2]

From Julie Ault and Martin Beck, "No-Stop City High-Rise: A Conceptual Equation." Bienal de São Paulo, 2010. Exhibition vitrine text.

[1] J. G. Ballard, quoted in *J. G. Ballard: Quotes*, ed. V. Vale, Mike Ryan (San Francisco: RE/Search Publications, 2004), p. 205. [*Speed: Visions of an Accelerated Age*, 1998]

[2] Ibid., p. 208. [*High-Rise*, 1975]

Preschool: My favorite lunch was **Morton's Macaroni & Cheese**, an individual serving that started out frozen and got baked to crusty-topped perfection. **A&P** brand was second choice. **Howard Johnson's** made a larger-size tin for sharing, but I didn't like to share. I wanted the consistency of knowing exactly how much I would have so I could plan each ecstatic bite. And **Hojo's** version was lumpier and less cheesy. I ate macaroni and cheese every day my mother let me.

Grade school: Mom packed a tuna sandwich for me day in and day out and gave me change to buy a half-pint of **Hood's** milk and some cookies or nabs at school. I switched off between **Nabisco's Nutter Butter Creme Patties** (the flat cream patty filled with real peanut butter—far preferable to the peanut-shaped cookie sandwich version), **Oreos, Peanut Butter Nabs, Cheddar Cheese Nabs**, and **Sunshine Biscuits' Vienna Finger Sandwiches**. But just thinking about the tuna mixed with mayonnaise without salt or pepper jammed between two slices of soggy misshapen bread sitting in my lunch box all morning made me sick. So I tossed the sandwiches. I was paranoid I'd get caught if I threw them out at school—too many eyes watching. Instead I carried the sandwich around with me all day in order to hide it at home under my brother's bed or in his closet. Not until years later did Mom start coming across unidentifiable dark-colored items when cleaning closets and the boxes under Brian's bed. (She was not a frequent housecleaner.)

From "Lunchtime Timeline: Some Brands I Have Loved." In *Lunch Break Times— Bay Area Edition*. Ed. Sharon Lockhart, p. 16. San Francisco: San Francisco Museum of Modern Art, 2011. Exhibition publication.

Had you not read or heard James Benning describe his film *casting a glance* (2007) prior to watching it, you'd likely assume that the sixteen dates that delimit its chronological structure and herald its constellation of eighty one-minute shots made at *Spiral Jetty* indicate when they were filmed. Each group of shots is introduced with a date, starting with April 30, 1970, which marks the jetty's beginning, and ending with May 15, 2007. The fact that the imagery is in fact the result of Benning's visits between 2005 and 2007 is not apparent in the film.

Benning claims it was not his intention to fool people into thinking he had been filming *Spiral Jetty* for thirty-seven years; he characterizes the conflation of chronologies as "a metaphor for history, a metaphor on time." Nonetheless some viewers find the designated time span confusing or feel hoodwinked when they realize the discrepancy. Others walk away in awe of what they believe to be the filmmaker's durable commitment to recording the jetty. For those who follow Benning's work closely, the superimposition of time frames—thirty-seven years, eighteen months, and eighty minutes—is far more artful and complex than a ploy; it is a valuable methodological manifestation of his persistent investigation into time, duration, and landscape.

From "4195.6 feet: Geography of Time." In *Ever Ephemeral: Remembering and Forgetting in the Archive*. Malmö: Signal Center for Contemporary Art and Inter Arts Center, 2011. Exhibition handout.

Julie Ault: Last night I read this letter that Felix sent to you in 1993, which at the time accompanied the gift of a clock. Until I read it, I had not consciously been thinking about the emotional content of reassembling the group of clocks. I've been mostly focused on the practicalities. The letter begins, "This is not a clock. It's more than just a machine that marks time," and ends, "To more time." It threw me into an emotional state, which was not how I'd planned to begin our conversation.

One interpretation of Felix collecting "optimistic clocks" the last couple years of his life is that he was buying time. But I never liked that explanation, in part because it doesn't reconcile with Felix as I knew him. Perhaps the clocks were not amulets so much as they were beautiful, tough objects that fed his process of working through the complex relationships to time, which the conditions he was living in, and with, brought forward. Perhaps the clocks were about facing time. Diagramming a situation of no escape. You can't ignore time when you have a dozen clocks on the wall.

What led me to regather the clocks was the desire to see them together again, and generate an occasion to recollect our memories of thinking through what to do with Felix's things when he died, specifically his books, the clocks, and the toys he collected. I'd like to revisit our decisions to disperse those things as we did and reflect on how they sit with us fifteen years later. There is also a desire to symbolically stage a reunion of community that was united around Felix and is now diffused, although particular bonds remain active.

Andrea Rosen: The movement between emotionality and objectivity you are talking about is a really essential part of this dialogue, because these positions were always fused in Felix's work. The work is a guiding force, or example, in that it imbues something with one's own personal emotionality but at the same time allows it to be stripped of anything personal in order that it might have some greater existence. . . .

I think we used Felix as our example when we made those
decisions about his things, which is to say, it's not that the clocks
weren't imbued with meaning, it's not that you can't read them
as being about holding on to time, it's not that anyone shouldn't
have considered them precious or representational. But Felix
set up an agenda. No matter how essentially private or however
much something is saturated with emotional content, the only
thing you can do for that to continue is to give it up. Felix set
an agenda for us.

From conversation with Andrea Rosen. In *Time Frames*, n.p. Malmö: Signal
Center for Contemporary Art and Inter Arts Center, 2011. Exhibition publication
for *Ever Ephemeral: Remembering and Forgetting in the Archive*.

Difference is where things get interesting. Difference was at the heart of Group Material's practice in terms of both process and projects. Different perspectives in dialogue, various methods informing and building on one another, a repertoire of diverse forms, and different media rubbing up against one another. But compatible intentionality in the larger sense bonds the efforts and differences.

While divergence was often a building block in the group, I wouldn't say conflict is categorically productive. It depends on what kind of conflict and how it is addressed and worked with by disagreeing parties and by the group at large. Group interrelations are sometimes blunt and sometimes incredibly subtle. In the earliest versions of Group Material, there were conflicts that could have been put to productive use but instead devolved into anger and alienation, mostly out of immaturity, egoism, and insensitivity. In later versions, conflicts sometimes went unarticulated and unexamined within the group as a whole, which was also detrimental. Suppression can undermine the dynamic.

Too much conflict can be exhausting and too much agreement can de-energize. This doesn't mean there has to be some happy medium or ultimate equilibrium, but it is essential to figure out effective methods to deal with these directions in context. There are so many cofactors at work in collaborative process, including moods.

From an unedited version of interview by Transformazium. In *Open Engagement*. Ed. Jen Delos Reyes, p. 20. Portland: Portland State University, 2011. Conference program.

For several years, Group Material was rather unhistorical,[129] not quite like the carefree beasts and children Nietzsche conjured but mostly unaware of being in history or of having one, capable only of being "honest."[130] Over time, historical consciousness took form in each of us for various reasons and it solidified in the group as a whole. The salient trigger was the AIDS crisis and the close-up witnessing of its casualties. Historical perception took hold in the larger sense of social development. Waking up to the "bad news" of History, we perceived a pileup of events colliding in the AIDS crisis, which seemed like a slow-motion disaster.[131] The group responded with no less than seven projects between

[129.] Cofounder Tim Rollins was never "unhistorical."

[130.] See Friedrich Wilhelm Nietzsche, "On the Use and Abuse of History for Life" (orig. published 1874), translated by Ian Johnston, revised edition, 2010. Accessed from http://records.viu.ca/~johnstoi/nietzsche/history.htm. (An art historian friend who enthusiastically recommended this translation, which she considers "far superior to the one in book form," directed me to this version.) "For the man says, 'I remember,' and envies the beast, which immediately forgets and sees each moment really perish, sink back in cloud and night, and vanish forever. In this way the beast lives unhistorically. For it goes into the present like a number without any odd fraction left over; it does not know how to play a part, hides nothing, and appears in each moment exactly and entirely what it is. Thus, a beast can be nothing other than honest." Hayden White clarifies, "In reality Nietzsche believed that human forgetting is quite different from animal oblivion." Hayden White, *Metahistory: The Historical Imagination in Nineteenth-Century Europe* (Baltimore: Johns Hopkins University Press, 1973), p. 7.

[131.] [Paul] Ricoeur quotes Walter Benjamin's description of the angel confronting the past in Paul Klee's *Angelus Novus*, "His face is turned toward the past. Where we perceive a chain of events, he sees one single catastrophe which keeps piling up wreckage upon wreckage and hurls it in front of his feet. The angel would like to stay, awaken the dead, and make whole what has been smashed. But a storm is blowing from Paradise; it has got caught in his wings with such violence that the angel can no longer close them. The storm propels him into the future to which his back is turned, while the pile of debris before him grows skyward. This storm is what we call progress." "Memory, History, Forgiveness: A Dialogue between Paul Ricoeur and Sorin Antohi," March 10, 2003, pp. 499–500, accessed at http://www.janushead.org/8-1/Ricoeur.pdf.

1989 and 1991, including exhibitions, a bus advertisement, a
publication project distributed over eleven art magazines, and
a sound installation.[132] . . .

A secondary strata of historical awareness coincided: group
self-consciousness of its own "history." The realization of being
in history and having chronology—a career so to speak—subtly
disrupted the group's process, and threw a monkey wrench into
its rhythm. Due to these notions of local and larger history, the
fresh, "honest," aspiring tone of the group's work deflated to
some degree. For example, conceptualizing a multiform four-
part project on democracy (albeit crisis in democracy), with minimal irony, would not have been possible if not for the group's
idealistic belief in cultural practice—in our practice—to impact
the social present. Somewhere between working on the first part
of *Democracy* (Dia Art Foundation, 1988), entitled *Education and
Democracy*, and the last, *AIDS & Democracy: A Case Study*, a
change in undercurrent was palpable.[134] The slide into awareness
of "having a history" is difficult to pinpoint and describe, but
for the group, it seemed to go hand in hand with the urgency
and death-toll environment related to AIDS. By then, Group
Material had existed for ten years, so it is likely that hitting the
decade limit sparked realization and nervousness. (It's been ten
years! Now what do we do?)

From "Remembering and Forgetting in the Archive: Instituting 'Group Material'
(1979–1996)," pp. 152–53. PhD diss., Malmö Faculty of Fine and Performing Arts,
Lund University, 2011.

[132] See "Chronicle" section of *Show and
Tell: A Chronicle of Group Material*,
ed. Julie Ault (London: Four Corners
Books, 2010), pp. 156–89.

[134] *Democracy*, four installations and town
meetings: *Education and Democracy,
Politics and Election, Cultural Participa-
tion*, and *AIDS & Democracy: A Case
Study*, Dia Art Foundation, New York,
September 15, 1988–January 14, 1989.
Followed by *Democracy: A Project by
Group Material*, ed. Group Material
and Brian Wallis, Discussions in
Contemporary Culture, no. 5 (Seattle:
Bay Press; New York: Dia Art Founda-
tion, 1990).

Corita's exceptional qualities are potentially narrowed as her work is established in the art field. Her serigraphs qualify as fine art and can therefore enter the account of modern art that curators and museums tell through art objects. Only rarely does that narration extend to address generative social contexts and ephemeral activities. The IHC [Immaculate Heart Community] and larger sociopolitical environment Corita worked in get invoked in press write-ups but are usually not visible in tandem with the presentation of her prints. Corita's crucial context is obscured—perhaps unintentionally, simply by retrofitting her prints into survey shows and museum collections under the header Pop art. In time, context may be altogether lost as they move about, accompanied by an increasingly simplified blurb about their maker, revised repeatedly to incorporate the styles of hosting institutions. Of course, this danger is not specific to Corita but potentially applies to all art. However in her case there seems to be a lot to lose.

On the other hand, Corita changes and complicates the discourse of Pop—which has been something of a done deal—and of postwar art history. American Pop art is almost exclusively the domain of male artists, including Rauschenberg, Johns, Hamilton, Warhol, Oldenburg, and Lichtenstein. (I am frequently asked if Corita knew the work of Andy Warhol. I'm sure she did, but I often wonder, did Warhol know the work of Sister Corita?) Furthermore, Corita's inclusion in the formal discussion of recent art history, which I must add is neither consistent nor assured in the long-term, highlights previous exclusionary modes and therefore fissures historical narrative. One wonders, what else has been marginalized and barred from the grand story of art as told by objects and approved practices? How hermetic is the canon? Can it be expanded? What does it take to do so? Authorized history is challenged by the reemergence of what has been omitted, again and again.

From "Entering the Canon, Expanding Art History." *September* (Portland Institute for Contemporary Art), no. 8. Ed. Anna Gray and Ryan Wilson Paulsen (2011): n.p. Exhibition newspaper.

It is difficult to identify where an association of ideas or interests begins, and it is just as complicated to pinpoint ending. Chronology is not much help. A chronology can start or end anywhere. It can extend in either direction indefinitely, depending on the scope of its frame(s) of reference. Storyline. Lifeline. Timeline. History. All open to reformulation. The linear appearance of chronology is deceptive, as is the perception that time flows from one direction to another. Physicists and philosophers widely agree that "the flow of time" is a creation of consciousness that we rely on for order.

Chronology and tense are inspected, analyzed, disarranged, and played with in *Ever Ephemeral*. A labyrinthine set of frictions that unfold in the archive is awakened here as well: between past tense and present tense, between remembering and forgetting, between completion and continuance, between the enduring and the ephemeral. The diffusion of *Ever Ephemeral* across two venues is meant to infuse its experience with recollection. A game of tag is set in motion as the exhibited constellation lays open innumerable relationships between archiving, memory, history, and narrative.

From "Ever Ephemeral." In *Ever Ephemeral: Remembering and Forgetting in the Archive*. Malmö: Signal Center for Contemporary Art and Inter Arts Center, 2011. Exhibition handout.

Tim Rollins: We also completely believe in the revolutionary power of beauty. We want to make objects that are solid and very physically present and generate this magic sense of security. Coming from families where everything is so uncertain: friends don't last, dads don't last, usually the only anchor is the mother, and because of the pressure she's part crazy half the time! But the making of the work is highly performative, though most of the action occurs in the mind. The dialogue, the perpetual laughter. K.O.S. is a team, and teams by their very nature like to compete. The issue is that we are not competing to be the best artists in the art world. We are competing against a history that has tended to exclude folks like us. I know you know about the Shakers in Maine. Have you been to their compound and farm lately?

Julie Ault: Oh God, Shaker Village. My favorite thing there is the massive tombstone that marks the surrounding pasture, inscribed with "Shakers." No names or dates, just "Shakers." Now that's collectivity! My other favorite thing was the drive to Sabbathday Lake from New Gloucester, where a lot of my family lived. I was always struck by how good the Shakers were at choosing the very best places. It's not just their building forms and arrangements, but the land itself that is also special. The breeze even feels different there. God, I sound so romantic, but it's like you always said, "You can take the girl out of Maine, but you can't . . ." That drive felt magical, like entering another world and leaving good old 1970s Maine mall culture (which I've got to admit, I also loved) behind.

From "Shakers," conversation with Tim Rollins. *Mousse* 30 (Fall 2011): p. 166.

The myth of America as "new world": imagining itself liberated from history but oblivious to its genocidal origin and repressive history in the making. Can a culture rooted in actively forgetting its own history do anything other than repeat itself?

Henry David Thoreau sought to "wake up the neighbors"[170] when the country was still in formation, slavery was overt, industrialization was fresh, and the paradoxical consequence of America was beginning to sink in. Ted Kaczynski began sounding the alarm against science-and-technology-driven society when he was in his early twenties. Benning's love/hate relationship with America runs through his life, evidenced in nearly forty years of work.

Two Cabins conjoins a variety of voices that induce the problematic of America—its false promise of freedom from and freedom to that simply will not square, a promise deeply embedded in its very conception that can never be satisfied. Apparitions of embodied autonomy populate the cabins: America as infinite producer of hope and despair and agitation. "Somehow I have to make an argument for 'a wanting of a utopia' that will surface under any conditions, with the idea that at least some people will always be able to reclaim their autonomy—even after it has been completely stripped from them."[171]

By authority of affinity, Benning has called this eclectic town meeting to order. Each attendee has a story to tell in a visual language of their making. The meeting is cochaired: Thoreau insists on our duty to the present and to individual conscience, gesturing to the pilgrim's life. Kaczynski sounds an apocalyptic forecast and a call to revolution, motioning to the primitive life. Discussion goes every which way: live in the mind, remake the world, go off on your own, make your own world; visions

---

[170] Thoreau wrote, "to wake my neighbors up." Quoted in Stanley Cavell, *The Senses of Walden* (Chicago: University of Chicago Press, 1972), p. 36.

[171] James Benning, conversation with the author, January 25, 2011.

proliferate of old times, other times, times to be. Benning, stand-
ing to the side, asks that we give consideration.

From "Freedom Club." In *Two Cabins by James Benning*. Ed. Julie Ault, pp. 142–43.
New York: A.R.T. Press, 2011.

Don't Be Yourself

In 1991, in need of change and disillusioned with what I perceived to be the art world's shallow relationship to sociopolitical issues, I enrolled at Hunter College. I wanted to go back to school and believed that as a returning student I might get something deeper out of it than I did when I was a teenager. Also, I was beginning to teach on the merits of my art practice, but I lacked a college degree.

I had been working as an artist for over a decade and had no interest in studying art. Instead, I gravitated toward political science, fueled by the fantasy of transitioning into politics proper, where I imagined I would find a more rigorous context of ideas as well as a keener sense of cause and effect than the one I experienced as an artist engaged with social issues. My outlook entering school that year was ridiculously idealistic.

Boy, was I surprised. The political-science division at Hunter College was conservative and appeared to be largely a feeder for the State Department. I felt out of place, but that unknown terrain was also strangely exciting. At the time, my personal style was scrappy thrift store: I wore a black leather jacket, which stood out in poli sci, particularly in the course called National Security, mostly populated by young men with perfect haircuts.

Initially I was confused about how to enter the dialogue and couldn't find my voice. I sensed the paradox of the returning student who at once knows too much and not enough. A greenhorn in live debate, I was more at home articulating politics in the spaces of art and exhibition making. Additionally, I was fed up with the black-and-white, us-versus-them mentalities that typified the Reagan-Bush years and the ongoing culture wars. I was questioning everything, including what I felt a connection with.

Realizing I was a clean slate in the environment, I decided to play with my identity and impulsively assigned myself an experiment: *don't be yourself, adopt another perspective and profess political views you disagree with.* The idea was purely intuitive. I would no doubt learn from advocating something I objected to, though I didn't know what.

My first major paper for the course on security was an in-depth discussion of the overthrow of Chilean president Salvador Allende written from a pro-US-government vantage. The paper captured the attention of the professor, who was also an editor of a Washington-based national-security journal. He graded it A-plus and invited me to his office for a chat.

"I'm having trouble reconciling your appearance with your ideological views," he began.

I played off his puzzlement. He let me know the unexpected paradox might hold some currency. "Are you interested in going to Washington?"

"Eventually," I replied.

But I wondered for the time being if he could organize an internship, for me. Anticipating the need to follow through unconditionally I switched my voter registration from Democrat to Republican the following day. And sure enough, in our next meeting he inquired about my political affiliation. "Republican," I answered firmly, looking him in the eye.

"I just want you to be comfortable with the internship placement," he replied.

This professor shepherded me through two internships with local Republican politicians, to which I would not have had access without his support.

In my first internship, working in a New York state senator's office, I was instructed to plow through various media reports and topical literature in search of problems that could be developed into research topics. If an issue seemed promising, the office would publish a report on the matter for the senator to present at a press conference, and he would garner media attention for his role as a community watchdog. Identifying the right type of theme was tricky; it had to be newsworthy and relevant to the senator's constituency, and a touch of controversy didn't hurt. School dysfunction, environmental protection, land-use debates, health care—all are fine, we research assistants were told. "But don't look into AIDS, unless it has to do with children. AIDS babies are OK."

My second internship, doing constituent services for a city councilman, was marginally more elevating. Some individuals' problems actually got solved: securing temporary housing for a family or providing someone with a new wheelchair, for example. But this work was primarily an exercise in navigating the intricate maze of city agencies in order to compel accountability. Some problems were extreme, like weeks of no heat in a city-owned apartment in the middle of winter. An individual citizen could complain all she wanted without result, but when the council member's office lodged a grievance, it got attention. Some issues, however, were impenetrable. For example, toxic emissions from a restaurant affecting the residents of a nearby apartment were surprisingly not the responsibility of *any* agency: the fumes fell into the crack between the purviews of the Department of Environmental Protection and the Department of Buildings.

I kept my utter shock over the cynical attitudes I encountered to myself. In all fairness, strategic thinking is the common core of electoral politics and is not special to the Republican party—although I didn't know this at the time. The experience of the Hunter poli-sci program and the internships deflated my idealism to the point that, ultimately, I concluded mainstream politics were more cynical than anything I'd experienced thus far in the cultural arena. I realized I was unwilling to distort myself enough to fit in and went running back to art.

And what had my self-assignment brought about? It was eye-opening and enlarging. Thinking beyond my professed set of beliefs and opinions and wrapping my mind around unfamiliar perspectives opened up new avenues of critical reflection. I learned to listen deeply to others as well as myself, to defer judgment and be less reactive and more analytic. I gained insight into how codes of identification and constituencies are constructed. I learned new rhetorical skills—how to express and advocate and argue from other points of view. It was like learning a new language. I matured. I thought about both politics and art more subtly than I had previously. And in the process, the naive idealism I had embarked on this project with transformed into something far more indeterminate and complex, productively informing my artistic practice and how I have thought ever since.

From *Draw It with Your Eyes Closed: The Art of the Art Assignment*, pp. 88–89. New York: Paper Monument, 2012.

The recovered letter from [Ted] Kaczynski's papers hit me like a brick, instantly undermining any illusion of being on solid, knowledge-based footing. The fact that Kaczynski had attempted to publicly link the bombs with antitech rationale radically altered the narrative I had speculatively (recklessly?) published. What else had I gotten wrong in my version of Kaczynski's difficult history?[5] How greatly had I also misconceived [Henry David] Thoreau and what erroneous and specious statements had I attached to his biography?[6] While knowing that the archive is random, and realizing that the range of writing about the

[5] The accuracy of many other issues I reiterated and represented vis-à-vis Kaczynski was thrown into question even earlier than encountering the *Examiner* letter, when I received an angry letter from him in response to the printout of the finished essay I'd forwarded. Kaczynski's correspondence detailed the problems of certain statements I'd made while noting that it would take way too much of his time to address all the errors in depth, as there were so many.

Despite the fact that I had been corresponding with Kaczynski for about nine months, I purposely had not run a draft of the essay by him in advance of its publication, because I believed independence and a degree of objectivity were necessary for my interpretive portrayal to be accepted as credible. I had not asked Kaczynski any questions specific to the content of my essay, and I did not quote from his letters or mention in the book that he and I were corresponding.

By mentioning our still-ongoing correspondence here, I invoke yet another set of documents that poten-tially adds to Kaczynski's chronicle. Although I consider the letters private, I don't know that I will always. Furthermore, Kaczynski periodically forwards copies of his correspondence to the Labadie Collection, where unless they have been restricted by Kaczynski, letters are made available to the public upon request after the Labadie redacts the originals for privacy, blacking out names and other identifying information.

[6] My concern didn't extend to [James] Benning in the same way, as the book is a collaboration between us, and because Benning had responded to and corroborated what I composed about him during my process of writing the essay. I don't mean to suggest that verification from the subject is undisputable truth. Historical representation requires balancing first-person, primary, and secondary sources among other references, both lasting and ephemeral. The double standard in my working relationship with the two living subjects of the book, Benning and Kaczynski, is now conspicuous to me.

Unabomber case veers from the scholarly to the sensational, and that Thoreau's biographies encompass abundant mythologizing, I nonetheless did what people engaged in historical inquiry frequently do—rely on and extrapolate from the record.

I have no doubt that the revealed error detailed here is but one instance of the latent surprises embedded in all modes of historical representation.

From "Addendum: The Recuperated Document." In *Afterlife: a constellation*, Whitney Biennial 2014. Whitney Museum of American Art, New York, 2014. Exhibition wall text, expanded from "Addendum." In *Freedom Club (Bootleg version booklet)*. Ed. Amy Zion, n.p. Annandale-on-Hudson, NY: Center for Curatorial Studies, Bard College, 2012.

Marvin Taylor: I have to ask this question because I'm curious about it. Does the archive tell the truth about Group Material? [*Ault chuckles.*] And I know that's a totally loaded question.

Julie Ault: Yes. The archive tells a lot of truths about Group Material. I suppose that's one of the fears that have to be confronted: what kind of story do you put out? And how? You know, I guess the fear is really about the violence of history writing. And making an archive is a form of history writing. It's not just because a book extends from the archive. That's not only the history writing but also the formation of the archive itself. You know, throwing this out, keeping this. I mean, I really kept everything. There was nothing that I threw out while cohering the archive from what I had saved. I don't know whether Doug Ashford cherry-picked or not. I somehow doubt it. But the material that Doug gave to the archive had a lot more intermingling of personal notes and things, so he probably did have to make some separations.

I think the archive tells some truths about Group Material, for sure. *Many* truths. But of course, you have to take it all with a grain of salt, because almost anything in the archive could be contested. Working on the book involved finding contradictions and trying to—not exactly reconcile things, but say, Okay, this says this; this says that. I don't remember either one, or, maybe, I remember what happened differently. The archive produces questions and is interesting, I think, for what is omitted and for its absences. And at the same time, you know, another little piece of paper might clarify something or unlock a mystery. I mean, there are so many intangibles of the practice that are not archived, intangibles of the process of the group, right? And those things are not there. So the truths are limited, frankly.

From interview by Marvin Taylor. In *Art Spaces Archives Project*, last modified September 2012, http://as-ap.org/oralhistories/interviews/interview-julie-ault-founding-member-group-material.

AIDS Timeline . . . sought at once to contextualize the AIDS crisis and to create a context itself—a didactic exhibit environment that examined recent events to account for present conditions, with the hope of influencing what was to come.

Agency was our horizon, and history—not only that of the 1980s, but history as continuum extending from earlier than 1979 and going on indefinitely. Chronology as guiding device set a linear horizon and performed an anchoring purpose, acting as a focal point from which viewers' perspectives could venture. Within such a setup, the horizon is endowed with the double function of systematizing and releasing information. The horizon opened views to what was above and below the timeline. It opened views to the larger set of conditions articulated by the arrangement of information brought into narrative armature, to reveal the far-reaching associations between political and cultural events that render the historical period legible.

From Julie Ault and Doug Ashford, *AIDS Timeline*, 100 Notes, 100 Thoughts: Documenta Series, no. 32, p. 3. Ostfildern: Hatje Cantz, 2012.

What does thinking in terms of research mean for your self-understanding as an artist?

It indicates being in a state of unending inquiry. Inquiry and growth are not temporally bounded, which means that formal manifestations of a particular investigation, such as exhibitions, writings, publications, and books, are not end points. For me, research terrain is typically tangled in process as it expands and contracts, goes awry, spirals out of control, distills, opens up again, unravels, and so on. The communicative forms produced along the way are temporary materializations of long-term investigations. Unlike the shape-shifting lead-up, they freeze the configuration of ideas and methods and material at a given time. Such productions are part of the inquiry process, perhaps even contrivances to punctuate or frame a period of research. But my engagement does not stop there. This is why I sometimes remain involved with a subject matter for years or decades, manifesting findings in different forms and with shifting perspectives over time.

From interview by Jan Kaila and Henk Slager. In *Doing Research: Writings from the Finnish Academy of Fine Arts*, no. 3. Ed. Jan Kaila and Henk Slager, pp. 57–58. Helsinki: Finnish Academy of Fine Arts, 2012.

"Have you seen my Mondrian drawing?" We went into the kitchen. He grabbed the frame facing the wall next to the sink and held it up so I could see it, though there was no light to speak of. Neither the fact that Martin Wong owned a work by Piet Mondrian nor that he stored it close to splashing water in his sixth-floor walk-up apartment in a run-down building on New York's pregentrification Lower East Side was incongruous. There, at 141 Ridge Street in apartment nine, Martin painted incessantly.

In Martin's private cosmos, cultural expression from distant eras and origins cohabited nonchalantly. There were Chinese blue-and-white porcelain stools to sit on and a drop cloth–*cum*–rug to catch wayward paint. Valuable ceramic figurines, books, and cartoon toys stood on every surface. Works of fellow artists that Martin had bought or traded for were interspersed with prints by Utagawa Kuniyoshi and his own paintings on the walls. Tags by graffiti-writer friends covered the refrigerator. In spite of the treasured objects throughout, the place was primarily for painting, so it was pretty messy.

In his collecting activities and in his art, Martin embodied a multiplicity of passions: Chinese ceramics, the paintings of Thomas Eakins and Winslow Homer, calligraphy, archers' thumb rings, children's lunchboxes, Mickeys and Minnies and Donalds, sign language, astronomical constellations, graffiti, Loisaida, the writing and person of Miguel Piñero, men in prison, firefighters, Chinatown.

From "Some Places It Will Always Be Eureka and in Eureka It Will Always Be Valentine's Day," In *Martin Wong: I·M·U·U·R·2.* Ed. Julie Ault, Daniel Buchholz, Heinz Peter Knes, Christopher Müller, and Danh Vo, p. 5. Berlin: Galerie Buchholz; Cologne: Walther König, 2013.

Gentrifying real-estate machinations go hand in hand with the growth, decay, migration, and conversion of NYC's art districts—SoHo, the East Village, Chelsea, Williamsburg, the Lower East Side, and so on. By the time [Martin Wong's] *The Last Picture Show* took place at the legendary Semaphore Gallery's final short-lived incarnation on Greene Street (1986–1987), director Barry Blinderman had closed both his original gallery on West Broadway (1980–1986) and Semaphore East (1984–1986) on Avenue B. Martin Wong had held a solo exhibition in each. Were his powerful storefront paintings also metaphors for yet another dying environment he held dear?

A series of places and the lived experiences in and around them. A context of concurrences. An era. Eras end constantly. Sometimes an era comes to an end because of massive change, sometimes by degree, and sometimes inconspicuously. Now and then it happens with the death of a single person.

From *Not only this, but "New language beckons us."* Ed. Andrew Blackley. New York University Fales Library and Special Collections, New York, 2013. Exhibition vitrine text.

Active Recollection: Archiving "Group Material"

Each person who sits down to write faces not a blank page but his own vastly overfilled mind. The problem is to clear out most of what is in it, to fill huge plastic bags with the confused jumble of things that have accreted there over the days, months, years of being alive and taking things in through the eyes and ears and heart. The goal is to make a space where a few ideas and images and feelings may be so arranged that a reader will want to linger awhile among them. . . . But this task of housecleaning (of narrating) is not merely arduous; it is dangerous. There is the danger of throwing the wrong things out and keeping the wrong things in.[1]
—Janet Malcolm

When the New York–based artists' collaborative Group Material disbanded in 1996, I continued its representation through live narration and writings and responded to inquiries on a case-by-case basis. As the only founding member who remained until its conclusion, I felt a responsibility to keep recounting the group's practice. Long-term member Doug Ashford did likewise. Group Material's cultural practice was temporal, and the forms employed were ephemeral. When the group ceased its activities, I was intent on preserving its ephemerality and *not* becoming history. Fearing a revisionist encapsulation in which conflicts and contradictions of collaboration are resolved in

[1] Janet Malcolm, *The Silent Woman: Sylvia Plath and Ted Hughes* (New York: Vintage, 1995), p. 205.

their representation, I resisted our work being defined or objectified in a monograph by an art historian, and reserved the right to cohere our history at some future point.

Following a decade of active narration, I realized it was time to relinquish responsibility and control, and address Group Material's history with lasting effect. I needed to confront the material traces that had infiltrated every closet, cabinet, and spare spot in my apartment, as well as the psychic traces that permeated memory. Collecting material saved by other group members as well, particularly the substantial amount of material saved by Doug Ashford, and joining it all together in an archive would permit access to Group Material in a more coherent way than had been possible before and open the door for further historical representation.

Tackling the mission of recuperating Group Material involved gathering and organizing the pool of material to constitute the archive, and simultaneously distilling from that body of information to make a book. While formalizing the archive, we sought to make Group Material public anew; the process was also conceived as a laboratory in which to investigate the logic, structure, implications, and practice of an archive. I spent several months processing the material in its soon-to-be-permanent home at the Downtown Collection at New York University: handling, reading, and looking at every paper, image, and item; taking notes, cross-referencing, recollecting, and reflecting.[2] The more I reviewed the more deeply I understood the malleable and fallible nature of memory, and memory repeatedly threw documentary fact into question. Alternatively edified and mystified, the experience demonstrated the utter insecurity of the categories subjective and objective.

[2] The Group Material Archive in the Downtown Collection can be viewed by appointment: Fales Library and Special Collections, Elmer Holmes Bobst Library, 70 Washington Square South, New York, NY 10012, USA. Email: fales.library@nyu.edu. Phone: (212) 998-2596.

Looking back, I realize while telling the story of Group Material these past years I had unwittingly told some lies. This discovery occurred when encountering information in files that I had long since blotted from memory. Surprised, I read on, and the divide between recollection and fact expanded. Certain retrieved information was basic while some signaled that Group Material was much more complex and debatable than I had meanwhile fabricated. It seems I had convinced myself that the streamlined storyline, which I repetitiously recounted for years, was accurate. My live narrations had fossilized into memorized short, medium, and long versions of the story. I repeatedly activated "habit-memory" and, in the process, obstructed active recollection, which makes it possible to "remount the slope of our past," and forge new relationships and meanings.[3]

Philosopher Paul Ricoeur reminds us that active recollection, or what he calls "recollection memory," involves recognition, which memory out of habit does not.[4] Habitual memory exists in a mental filing cabinet, accessible on demand with the right call number.[5] Rupturing that dead-end circuit required purposely entering memory of a different order, "present memory," as part of the larger process of apprehending, relearning, and gaining fresh insight into Group Material through archiving and publishing.[6]

---

[3] Paul Ricoeur, *Memory, History, Forgetting,* trans. Kathleen Blamey and David Pellauer (Chicago: University of Chicago Press, 2004), p. 431. Ricoeur recounts two forms of memory Henri Bergson theorized in *Matter and Memory*, "habit memory, which is simply acted out and lacks explicit recognition, and recollection memory, which is not without declared recognition."

[4] Ibid., p. 336.

[5] "Memory no longer consists in recall-ing the past but in actualizing what has been learned and stored in a mental space. In Bergsonian terms, we have crossed over to the side of habit memory." Ibid., p. 62.

[6] I have borrowed the term *present memory* from the title of a 2010 work by artist Alejandro Cesarco to suggest, in this instance, memory that is present that takes place in the present and makes present or represents the past, simultaneously, which can happen with live narration.

Of course, documents and artifacts are not intrinsically truth telling either; they are fragmentary and disconnected from context. Archives set the stage for history writing, yet they can mislead and even lie through omission. Essential pieces of information, which might answer questions and redirect research, are not necessarily tangible or archived.

Each aspect of cohering the archive and making the book *Show and Tell: A Chronicle of Group Material* (Four Corners Books, 2010) embodied specific and abstract purpose. A set of vexing questions fueled the work. How does bringing documentation together imply shaping history and writing history? How do artifacts—whether material or information—communicate? Can contexts be, in effect, communicated? What archival structure and practices will animate and complicate without overdetermining meanings? What tense is the archive? Where does the archive end? What can the collective subjective do when given the chance to write its own history? What is gained and lost in the process of subjecting ephemeral activities to conservation, and inducting them into history? What kind of suitable forms can be shaped to embody the historicizing processes, gathered knowledge, and diverse purpose that drive this inquiry? How to make what is missing evident as a layer of historicizing? How does the subjective transform the material to a public sphere without manipulating it? Can one effectively challenge history writing while writing history?

Answering the question: "Why did things happen like that and not otherwise?" requires turning past events into a "followable story," which historian Hayden White distinguishes from historicizing a *completed* story. Chronicles are capable of telling followable stories, whereas timelines endeavor to answer other questions, which call for judgment: "What does it all add up to?" "What is the point of it all?"[7]

---

[7] Hayden White, *Metahistory: The Historical Imagination in Nineteenth-* *Century Europe* (Baltimore: Johns Hopkins University Press, 1973), p. 7.

Chronicles and timelines both function as narrative armatures. Both modes are linear at heart, but the informational reach of the timeline format is potentially more global as it encompasses multiple lines of inquiry and is capable of bringing seemingly incompatible information into confrontation. Timelines make larger explanation and historical analysis possible. Chronicles import events and sequence. Chronicles record rather than historicize.

Because Group Material had used the timeline format as an exhibition structure on occasion, the idea of organizing the book as a timeline of Group Material's history was briefly contemplated, but was rejected for that same reason—it seemed potentially trite when set alongside the group's timeline exhibitions.[8] Group Material conceived of a timeline exhibition as a mapping scheme capable of generating immersive diagrams of past events and potential readings of cause and effect within which viewers could navigate constellations of information and in the process formulate history. Yet graphic and printed timelines tend to reduce and level information on a unified seamless platform, indicating that narratives have already been established into consumable, compressed history lessons.

As the above questions that stimulated reopening the case of Group Material indicate, the inclination was to avoid pronouncements such as "This is what Group Material was all about." To this end, a chronicle structure seemed ideal.

Show and Tell's main section comprises reprinted documents and images, with a guiding text running throughout. The chronicle takes its ingredients and methods from the archive,

---

8. Group Material employed the timeline format as a research and structuring device for two exhibition projects. The first was *Timeline: A Chronicle of US Intervention in Central and Latin America* (1984), PS1, New York, and the second was *AIDS Timeline* (1989), Matrix Gallery, University Art Museum, University of California at Berkeley, which had subsequent versions.

which embodies both private and public material. The making
of the group as a specific context along with its structure and
process is inseparable from its public creations, yet the bulk
of existing representation focuses on the latter. *Show and Tell*
widens the focus to include conveyance of internal workings in
each layer of material that forms the book and stresses aspects
of the collaboration that would have otherwise been invisible.

Group Material comes to life through the archive. Working
with the material, I was struck by the vividness and changing
character of internal correspondence, minutes of meetings, exhibition proposals, and press releases produced by the group. Emotional intensity is palpable in early communiqués: proposals and
press releases are bombastic, topics and debates of the times are
glimpsed through language, and graphic design bespeaks period
styles. A selection of documents is reprinted in their original
form and scale in *Show and Tell*. They are valued as "original language," which vividly conveys what we perceived we were doing
at the time far better than something written from the distance
of time would, whether by someone inside or outside the group.
This material would commonly be considered source material for
writing rather than substance for presentation. By design, the
book encourages that the documents be regarded as primary texts
rather than ancillary illustrations. This method situates readers
in the archive, inviting a multiplicity of interpretation.

Contradictory evidence is at the heart of the archive and
prominently figures in this portrayal of Group Material.
A four-page incendiary letter titled "A PROPOSAL FOR
LEARNING TO GET THINGS OFF OUR CHESTS;
BEHAVIORS, DISCIPLINE AND OUR PROJECT,"
written by cofounder Tim Rollins to the group in 1980, is fully
reprinted alongside documents that represent a more harmo-
nious collaboration. Tim's letter rants and rails rhetorically.
It evidences major clashes in the group's first months, but it
also shows how seriously he regarded the collaboration and
articulates what was at stake for the group.

The guiding text that filters throughout the chronicle was conceived as a nonspecific voice imparting otherwise inaccessible circumstances, facts, and anecdotes alongside the archive materials. It represents a close reading and distillation of multiple documentation and composite memory. This text captions, reports, digresses, and discloses, coalescing subjective and objective knowledge into a seamless voice that augments the material. A depersonalized present-tense mode is used, intended to situate readers in the times of events and suggest collective subjectivity, distinct from first-person retrospection. Trains of information such as the continuities and discontinuities of the group's composition, conflicts and contradictions endemic to its process, and how Group Material structured itself and financed its work run throughout.

While reading through Group Material's files, I noted many interesting segments in all types of documents, initially regarding this as source material for the guiding text. The number of full documents that could be reproduced was limited by the book's budget, which led to creating a layer of diverse extracts varying in author, purpose, length, and style. Unified by typographic design treatment, these also filter throughout the chronicle.

Image-wise, snapshots portraying the various members and incarnations of the group, although in some cases there are no photographs, and formal installation photography of the collaborative's forty-five projects are presented on equal footing.

The chronicle's carefully designed formal system stresses all the material as primary. The book's visual tone builds on Group Material's aesthetic style. Analogous to the decentralized thematic exhibition format the group advanced, the chronicle is thought of as an exhibition space in the form of a book.

In his work to categorize history writing, White has pointed out that a key problem of the (objective) chronicle or chronology is the notion that events tell themselves, in lieu of a (subjective) narrator.[9] At first glance, the chronicle of Group Material does exactly that, given that artifacts, facts, and anecdotes are made present through themselves and by grammatically articulating the past as present. The archive shows itself, albeit through the prejudiced curatorial eyes of its participant interlocutor(s). Narration is not absent in *Show and Tell* and the narrator is conceived and configured as a "collective subjective," constituted by the group that once was, and a more abstract version of the amalgam Group Material, which is conjured to do the telling in the present.

The chronicle spotlights atmosphere; its close-range eye-level orientation conveys that the collaboration was serious and it was fun; a sociable context.[10] A photographic analogy is helpful: the book's perspective is akin to a ground-level, human-scale way of looking, while perspective situated in larger historical discourse is comparable to an aerial, bird's-eye view. Each method omits: the ground shot includes only glimpses of surroundings, the longer view makes it difficult to see what's happening close up—such as a social process.

Ricoeur distinguishes the effects of scale in history writing: "What can be seen on a large scale are the developing forces. But what can be seen on a small scale—and this is the lesson of microhistory—are the situations of uncertainty within which individuals . . . attempt to orient themselves. . . . Therefore, when you write macrohistory, you are more likely to work with determinisms, whereas when you work on microhistories, you have to engage indecisions, that is to say indeterminism."[11]

---

9. Hayden White, "The Value of Narrativity in the Representation of Reality," in *On Narrative*, ed. W. J. T. Mitchell (Chicago: University of Chicago Press, 1981), especially pp. 2–4.

10. The detailed data of the exhibition history near the book's end, of venues, institutions, places, participants, and collaborators, are coordinates that portray context and inscribe a larger field of action and social relations. The exhibition titles of documented work chart a compendium of concerns and objectives.

11. "Memory, History, Forgiveness: A Dialogue between Paul Ricoeur and

Emphasizing actions and dynamics at ground level seeks to highlight social process over effect and judgment. This emphasis works to create a multivalent space that can be engaged and projected into and out from, a space to harbor multiple points of entry and identification, and rouse interest, inspire imagination, critical consciousness, and analysis. Contemporaries who revisit the period through the lens of Group Material attend with their individual awareness and interests as well as with an expanse of cultural memory. Those who are less familiar or unfamiliar with Group Material's activity and context are invited in at eye level to witness actions and circumstances through recollection of evidence and memory, conveyed in a present-tense telling, which regenerates a fundamental sense of cultural agency.

Books tend to streamline material and position readers by imposing a point of view, that of the narrator. Framing or summarizing from a post-mode of narration can potentially short-circuit viewers' processes of discovery and conclude rather than extend Group Material in the process. *Show and Tell*'s chronicle is decentralized: it does not privilege one point of view—much like a decentralized Group Material exhibition environment in which there is no ideal view; all views are potentially ideal and multiple perspectives are spurred.

Revisionist and interpretive tendencies have been restrained in *Show and Tell* in favor of creating a useful documentary foundation and introduction to Group Material's archive. The organization of the archive and the response to that process through the book provide a platform and base interpretation to use, negotiate, and take issue with.

The modality used for the "present representation of absent, past things"[12] is dictated by purpose. Faithfully representing the

Sorin Antohi," March 10, 2003, p. 13, accessed at http://www.janushead .org/8-1/Ricoeur.pdf.

[12] Ricoeur, *Memory, History, Forgetting*, p. 138.

group (to ourselves) for the sake of articulation, conservation, mourning, and regeneration influenced the mode of *Show and Tell*. Cohering the archive in public, literally taking it out of our hands and making the book, is in part a formality for mourning the death of the group and regenerating the ideals that underwrote its course.

On the local level, faithful resemblance is tested through recognition, by ringing true. Do we recognize Group Material in this book? Does the depiction do justice to personal and collective memory? Do those who participated in and encountered Group Material's projects in real time recognize and recollect? Turning past events into "history" is only partly for those who remember. The prime social reason for reopening the case was to stimulate action in the present and future. Further affinity is aspired to. The seemingly opposing goals of being, on the one hand, recounted and, on the other hand, open-ended beckoned. Because *Show and Tell* inaugurates Group Material's "history," it has the ability to define what Group Material "was all about." Intentionality is implied in the details of the documentation presented, but it is not summarized retrospectively. The paramount intention to represent faithfully and generate affinity dictated the book's methods. In its collaborative essence, and through its exhibition practice, Group Material embodied decentralization as it created contexts in response to precise conditions, conflicts, and alliances. The objectives that guided Group Material to resist making declaratives in its practice in favor of fashioning multivocal forums guided the approach in the book. Avoiding historical contextualization invites a multitude of individual and social interpretations by the book's users, along their own lines of understanding, instead of prescribed ones, in essence, making it possible for readers to do the work of interpretation and historicizing themselves.

In the aftermath of cultural presence, any iteration of Group Material is by definition history. Interpretation is suffused in every moment of searching, curating, editing, assigning relevance, and connecting dots between documents that constitute research, including not least, presenting. However, *Show and Tell* stops short of overt interpretation as an explicit means. Group Material could be historicized more broadly in relation to intellectual and cultural turns and social trends, including postmodernism, multiculturalism, feminism, etc.; but such framing risks sacrificing its particular dynamics. Grounding Group Material's portrayal within larger social frameworks, which, at the time, appeared to be limitless but have since been bounded and periodized by historicization, is at odds with composing a historical representation to launch clearings so that social memory and imagination in its diversity might be generated. In *Show and Tell*, Group Material's status is meant to be protected as *untheorized historically*.[13]

Historical staging is blunt. Group Material would be one thing in relation to punk and another in relation to postmodernism or Conceptual art, the 1980s, or activism. Framing devices can be changed like backdrops in a photo studio, to change the figure's appearance in relation to different settings. Given that the group did not delimit its practice or definitively identify with any particular movement, ism, or classification, it would be somewhat arbitrary to fasten on to one historical scaffolding.

When local history is situated in or against a historicized context that is larger and preestablished as a subject/discourse, it is in danger of being absorbed. The larger configuration tends to "explain" the microhistory of a specific group of people and their experiences, decisions, and actions. The microhistory gets thematicized and rendered an illustration of a larger phenomenon. Because of the tendency of historical contextualization to function as explanation, the position taken rejected *all*

13. This was the stance I took as the book's editor and was not a group decision.

frameworks, to instead focus on one microhistory and its capacity to accentuate and register cultural conditions and change, through the lens itself.

Consider, for instance, were Group Material to be historicized by multiculturalism. As soon as the term is put forward, its potential to take over is expressed. It is true that Group Material was in itself heterogeneous and reflected various multiplicities in its exhibitions. But this was not because of "multiculturalism," it was because culture *is* multicultural. That society is made up of multiple cultures is an undeniable fact.[14] Culture was multicultural before the term *multiculturalism* was active in any arena.

Clearly I do not mean to diminish or denigrate any theoretical inquiry and articulation, or any lived experiences associated with multiculturalism, postmodernism, or feminism, etc., including my own. The impetus is to question the consequences of sweeping up the works and investigations of any artist, writer, or practitioner into periodizing models, intellectual debates, or social movements at the expense of their potential open-enddedness.

There is paradox in situating a practice that sought to "question the entire culture we have taken for granted,"[15] and the master narratives and dominant institutions of that culture, within an antigrand narrative, such as postmodernism—a "discourse of delegitimation."[16] In spite of its critical design, such

[14] I am speaking generally about the US.

[15] "Our project is clear. We invite everyone to question the entire culture we have taken for granted." Group Material inaugural statement, 1980. Reprinted in *Show and Tell: A Chronicle of Group Material*, ed. Julie Ault (London: Four Corners Books, 2010), p. 23.

[16] Referring to Lyotard's argument in *The Postmodern Condition* that the discourses of legitimation have failed, and then talking about the "grand narratives" proposed by Christian theology and Marxism, which have lost their credibility: "We are engaged, whether we like it or not, in a discourse of delegitimation." Ricoeur, *Memory, History, Forgetting*, p. 313.

discourse can function as an alternative account—a history of dissent, counterculture, and constellations of critical intellectual debate, which takes shape as a quasi-grand narrative of Opposition.[17] I do not mean to suggest that historians and theoreticians plan this course. Although Group Material sometimes portrayed culture as a battleground, for the most part it sought to cut across such a territorialized notion of the cultural economy and of society and to speak in terms of "for" rather than "against." In the long term, Group Material did not speak the vocabulary of opposition or dissent so much as participation, agency, and multiplicity. For Group Material to be recognized, it needs to reinforce itself. *Show and Tell* refuses to speak in terms of oppositions. The apparent dichotomies of dominant and marginal, culture and counterculture, left/right, righteous and corrupt, aesthetic and political, etc., lost their soundness over time in practice. On behalf of Group Material, *Show and Tell* takes a less contrast-driven stance. By refusing to affirm such disunion in representation, *Show and Tell* stays true to the group's history of lived experience and does not further replicate polarizing notions of culture.

From *Self-Organised*. Ed. Stine Hebert and Anne Szefer Karlsen, pp. 102–12. London: Open Editions, 2013.

---

17. "As microhistory has already verified, the initial benefit of a variation in scale is that it shifts the accent to the individual, familial or group strategies that call into question the presupposition of submission by social actors on the bottom rank to social pressures." Ibid., p. 218.

Carrie Mae Weems began a talk I attended at the Wadsworth
Atheneum in 1991 by telling a joke that made fun of Nancy
Reagan. The audience cracked up. She let us laugh long. Then
she told another joke, "How do you get a black man out of a tree?
You cut the rope." The place went silent. Carrie made her point;
humor depends on where you are sitting and how you identify
with who is being scorned.

In 1987–88 Carrie made a series of text-image works called
Ain't Jokin'. In one work, a beautiful young black woman averts
her gaze from the mirror in front of her, where a veiled apparition
holds up a silver star. "Looking into the mirror, the black woman
asked, 'Mirror, Mirror on the wall, who's the finest of them all?'
The mirror answers, 'Snow White, you black bitch, and don't you
forget it.'" This work caused many raised eyebrows and puzzled
looks hanging in my bedroom, especially when the building
superintendents or handymen passed through.

From "*Tell It to My Heart* Annotated." In *Tell It to My Heart: Collected by Julie Ault*.
Ed. Julie Ault, Martin Beck, Nikola Dietrich, Heinz Peter Knes, Rasmus Røhling,
Jason Simon, Scott Cameron Weaver, Danh Vo, and Amy Zion, p. 146. Ostfildern:
Hatje Cantz, 2013. Exhibition catalogue.

I must admit I feel a bit uneasy about the notion that the art I am
fortunate enough to live with constitutes, potentially, the "Julie
Ault collection." Accumulating artworks, artifacts, ephemera,
books, and so on has been an organic process rather than the
reflection of a conscious archiving instinct. Such constituents do,
however, act as building blocks of identity, as well as the tracings
of relationships and work contexts. Over time, the responsibility
to protect the material traces of ideas, people, practices, and contexts, even as they shift or disappear, has clarified into an active
motive. The works in "my collection" confront me continually,
just as the artists they are made by do, and have in the past.
They stand for relationships and for personal and public histories. And there is the pleasure of it all, the everyday delights and
challenges of living among the voices of those I most respect
and attend to.

From preface to *Tell It to My Heart: Collected by Julie Ault*. Ed. Julie Ault, Martin
Beck, Nikola Dietrich, Heinz Peter Knes, Rasmus Røhling, Jason Simon, Scott
Cameron Weaver, Danh Vo, and Amy Zion, p. 154. Ostfildern: Hatje Cantz, 2013.
Exhibition catalogue.

My artistic background in collaboration and exchange continues at the heart of my work. I first encountered Corita's prints while in transition from the collaborative structure I had worked in for sixteen years—Group Material—to embarking on a solo practice. Searching for role models during that professional shift, I found this woman of many talents, insights, causes, and networks. I felt affinity with Corita's collaborative spirit, and the community she was a part of. I was inspired by their creative drive in the face of oppressive authority structures, and by their courage to go their own way.

I admire Corita the teacher, Corita the artist, Corita the catalyst, and mostly, Corita's ability to fuse celebration, aesthetics, and critical consciousness in her practice of life and art. Corita is always timely. Her artistic and graphic innovations of decades ago speak freshly to current art, design, and social practices. Her political consciousness and antiwar stance connect with us right now. Corita's word-images tickle the mind and delight the eye as they speak across time, her voice nourishing the present.

From "In." In *Someday Is Now: The Art of Corita Kent*. Ed. Ian Berry and Michael Duncan, p. 100. New York: DelMonico Books; Munich: Prestel, 2013.

Russell and Karin loved coming to visit us in Joshua Tree and did so frequently. We had holidays there and many fine simple times sitting on the patio, alternating between reading, napping, and watching the views, seeing and sensing the light change throughout the day in tandem with the colors we were surrounded by, marveling over how incredibly bright the stars are at night, making and enjoying good meals together—actively looking forward to every meal is something Karin and I shared and talked about probably way too much—hanging out, relaxing, rejuvenating, sitting in front of the fire talking, going on gorgeous walks and breathtaking hikes. The only trick was getting Russell and Karin to arrive in Joshua Tree in time for the magic hour; usually they liked to stop at the Cabazon factory outlet mall on the way out and arrived on the cusp of sundown, with many treasures in tow. Karin took great pleasure in shopping and finding special items on sale. As an extension of this, every Joshua Tree visit involved the semiguilty pleasure of a trip to the Walmart in the next town. Russell and Karin would be reading heady literature one minute, hiking the next, and exuberantly racing through Walmart the following. Once we lost them at Walmart for what seemed an awfully long time, so we had them paged. "Will Russell and Karin please meet their friends at the front of the store?" A few minutes later, they appeared with an overflowing cart and big grins, flushed by tales of bargains galore.

Karin placed her enthusiasm carefully—in ideas, in art, in historical inquiry, in particular people, in good organizational practices, in hiking and Pilates, in certain foods, places, and other elements and rituals of daily life. She loved beauty and utility combined. Care and complexity are evident in everything Karin touched, in the exhibitions she created, the subject terrains she fashioned, the home she made with Russell. Karin loved talking shop and offering her responses to work seen and read. Karin was gifted with critical insight, passion, honesty, a subtle mind, and—when she wanted—diplomacy. These made her a wonderful intellectual partner, as well as an ideal viewer, reader, and advocate.

From "Karin Higa," memorial remarks, Hammer Museum, Los Angeles, December 8, 2013. In *Karin Higa*, pp. 78–79. Los Angeles: Russell Ferguson, 2015.

Julie Ault: I regard you as the author of the Downtown Collection. I've read the boilerplate description of what constitutes the collection, but I'm longing for a kind of director's cut about your intentions, purposes, and conceptual framing, and discussion of the implicit as well as the explicit criteria you used to both formulate and shape the collection. Do you consider yourself the author of the collection?

Marvin Taylor: For me, it's been a project: how can we take a scene that was deeply invested in institutional critique and document that scene in an institution without letting the institution completely take over and do all the things that institutions do once they get hold of material that is in some way critical of their very existence? Most repositories would just bring the materials in, catalogue them in the traditional ways, and the collections' energies and spirit would die the death of cataloguing, just like dried butterflies.

I chose not to do that. Instead, I chose to modify what archivists call the "documentary strategy" as much as possible rather than adopt the "connoisseurship strategy." I try to keep alive as much of the transgressive nature of downtown work as possible. (*Transgressive* is a word many people don't like, but the materials we have ask constantly, "Why are you doing this?" "What structure is informing how this is done?") I guess I would like to be thought of as the author who questions his authorial intent while actually building the collection; to be very conscious at every step of the kind of decisions I am making and the implications of those decisions.

From "Active Recollection: Marvin Taylor in Conversation with Julie Ault," New York: Whitney Museum of American Art, 2014. Exhibition handout for *Afterlife: a constellation*, Whitney Biennial 2014.

Julie Ault: I've been thinking about my own complicated relationship to past work—I get very anxious when I have to revisit or represent it. Some work feels far away and deep past—hard to connect to. Some work has been situational, motivated by context. And certain things feel right till today, and I think, "Oh, this is just how I would do that right now."

So I'm struck that you continually show works that were, in some instances, made long ago. Your work invariably comes afresh to me as a viewer and seems to speak to the present. This is striking—I've never encountered a work of yours that seems outdated, or that I regard as early or immature or old work. When I encounter your work I don't think about time or place beyond the present. I don't know how to account for this. It's rare.

Roni Horn: I've been told that by other people who have known the work over many years. I don't know how to account for it either. Maybe because I include the idea of its experience in the development of the work. This often means the architecture as well. But I really don't know.

It's one of the things that happens when I'm working, particularly on a large show, since these shows are as much about my life as they are about any viewer's experience. So, I will take work that was done a long time ago or that I haven't seen in a long time and put it in the context of the other work. I've found the new work helps me understand the older work and that retrospective reflection is prominent in the way I work.

From "Moving Water: The Flow of Roni Horn," conversation with Roni Horn. In *Roni Horn: Everything Was Sleeping as if the Universe Were a Mistake*, pp. 138–39. Madrid: Turner Libros, 2014. Exhibition catalogue.

Dishes, Diaries, and Cemeteries: Josephine Fountain Tufts

As a young girl, the person I was closest with was Aunt Jo, my great-aunt. I followed her around doing housework and picking vegetables in the garden. I learned to cook in Aunt Jo's kitchen, which was dominated by a mammoth wood-burning stove—the primary heat source for the two-story twelve-room farmhouse she lived in her entire life, along with her brother. Handmade quilts, homemade beds stuffed with down and feathers, and hot-water bottles filled from the kettle permanently lodged atop the stove supplied local warmth at bedtime. That stove must have been pretty large, in fact as in memory, since Aunt Jo managed to cook a giant turkey dinner with an impressive range of vegetable and side dishes, as well as a pantry full of pies, for twenty or so family members every Thanksgiving.

Aunt Jo's life revolved around her daily list. Written in ballpoint pen on a small unlined five-and-dime pad of paper, each page was a script of the chores she sought to complete that day—"vacuum living room," "laundry," "scrub sink," "dust upstairs bedrooms," "ironing," "pick berries," "mend dress," etc. She typically took two aspirin every four hours, coffee breaks at 10 and 3, and lunch at noon. There were consistent tasks of baking cookies, cakes, and pies, preparing breakfast, lunch, and supper, and shopping in town at the supermarket and Woolworth's. There were family visits and social calls on neighbors. There were holiday celebrations. There was church every Sunday, and in the dozen or so years of its existence during her lifetime—television in the evenings.

One day when I was twelve, Aunt Jo, wearing a roll of masking tape around her wrist and holding the Magic Marker she used to date the jars of fruit and vegetables she canned for winter, took me into the pantry. Opening every cupboard, she asked me what I wanted when she died, so she could put my name on the bottom of the things I chose. I knew exactly what I wanted, but was embarrassed to say. I must have given her an explanation as she let me off the hook—"I'm not sure, I'll tell you later," or "I don't want to think about that." The scene is both vivid and vague in my mind's eye. Whether it actually happened or is something I wished for or dreamed I can't be certain.

I was fourteen when Aunt Jo got sick and went in the hospital. My mother wouldn't let me go see her. She'd turned yellow, I was told—jaundice or hepatitis. She was dead soon after. She might have wondered why her great-niece, who was so devoted—the one she was tender with, who everyone said was "just like her," who slept near her in bed, the one whose chamber pot she emptied in the morning since most Maine nights were too cold to send a young girl to the outhouse, didn't come to see her as she lay dying. Or maybe she didn't. I have no idea then or now of Aunt Jo's interior life.

From necessity, Josephine Fountain Tufts was a workhorse, shouldering and grumbling, shouldering and grumbling. Family members were mostly complicit. "Mark my words," she confided, "they'll expect me to get out of the grave and wait on them at my funeral." I don't know if her prediction bore out, as I did not attend her funeral. Eager to protect me from pain and "negative things," my mother prohibited me from going. On numerous occasions, Aunt Jo asked me to plant a potato plant on her grave someday.

Aunt Jo sputtered incessantly about her brother, Uncle Carl. "That man," she'd say disdainfully as if the reasons for her contempt were self-evident, "that man; just look at him." Some time after she died, he also led me into the pantry so I could show him what I wanted and take "the damn stuff" with me. (Like all my maternal relatives, Uncle Carl was unsentimental. Come to think of it, so are the paternal ones.)

I chose the brightly colored metal tumblers they had used every day and some of the glass ones printed with flowers, as well as some decorated jelly jars, which used to be given complimentarily with the purchase of a tank of gas. I wanted two or three serving platters. And there was the small pitcher with blue flowers painted on it that I'd long coveted. When Uncle Carl reached for it, I was scared it would have someone else's name on the bottom, but it didn't. Most precious were Aunt Jo's everyday dishes, which I didn't dare use for forty years. When I finally began to last spring, I shattered a cereal bowl the first week. (Storing things that are "too good to use" is a family trait. After my grandmother died, we found one of her bureau drawers utterly stuffed with fine soaps and fancy packages of body powder—a half-century of gifts.)

Bent-over lame from digging graves at the town cemetery, Uncle Carl hobbled to the shed to get some boxes so I could cart away the dishes. With the transfer completed, he motioned to the jars lined up on the pantry counter—the year's bounty of his signature seriously sour pickles. Uncle Carl didn't waste pickles on people he didn't care for; offering a jar was telling. The routine was that you opened it on the spot and immediately ate one, grimacing against your will while exclaiming its tartness. Then you offered him one, fully anticipating the punch-line response—"I never touch the stuff"—followed by a yelp or hoot delivered as he limped back to the kitchen.

Or maybe he was already sitting in the rocking chair that was formerly the exclusive domain of his sister when you opened the jar. Uncle Carl's personal chair was nestled in the corner between the stove and a window that looked out onto the road. When he wasn't in the garden or at the cemetery, he was in that chair, talking to himself or whoever came by, watching the outside, or writing in his diary. For decades, he recorded the local facts at day's end—the weather, who came to visit, who drove up and down the road and how many cars had strangers at the wheel, hunting stories, the state of his garden, what was harvested, illnesses, deaths, news from neighbors, and so forth.

When Uncle Carl died, my mother's sister Aunt Dot, who had lived her whole life down the road from him, promptly got rid of all of his things without consulting a soul. Personal belongings, treasures of shared histories, things kept so long they became valuable antiques, and the 1930s kitchen table that was the heart of the house, painted an ethereal shade of light green. My mother and brother and I were horrified. Over and over, I asked her why she opted for going to the dump and calling the antique dealers instead of us—why we had no say in the dismantling of the environment that had such a powerful role in forming us. She always got defensive and a little cross, "Oh, I don't know. I don't know. I just did."

From *Afterlife: a constellation*. In Whitney Biennial 2014, Whitney Museum of American Art, New York, 2014. Exhibition wall text.

Liberace learned from Las Vegas and the copious use of reflective surfaces in casino design. The performer covered entire walls and rooms with mirrors, attaining the illusion of amorphous space, places to lose oneself—a form of magical privacy. In addition, mirrored areas transformed Liberace's home into a glamorous theater, placing himself and his intimates on display, and further populating the setting with ephemeral companions. The star attempted to outshine Versailles with what he termed "palatial kitsch," fashioning a lavish private concourse that he christened the Hall of Eternal Mirrors.

In 2013, one of Liberace's former Las Vegas homes went on the market due to foreclosure. I was inspired to find furtive walk-throughs and peeking-through-the-window tours online, along with vintage footage from when he lived there. Reflectivity seems to flow throughout the mansion. Entranceways are covered in mirrors, the hall of mirrors leads to mirrored double doors that open into a room with mirrored pillars and a mirrored ceiling. The vacant mansion and its multiplicity of reflections induce a poignant atmosphere of transience. Visual apprehension gets slippery in the setting. Ethereal reflections glide through the mirrored domains, in sync with their mortal counterparts.

The double edge of the mirror is its potential for vulnerability and, ultimately, disappearance. Reflection becomes the site of inexpugnable experience: a present tense of accumulated traces, in no particular order. Look at yourself in a mirror all your life, and you'll see death at work.[7]

From "Liberace's Mirrors: A Glimpse." In *PS: Jahresring 61: Jahrbuch für moderne Kunst.* Ed. Dominic Eichler and Brigitte Oetker, pp. 70–71. Berlin: Sternberg Press, 2014.

[7] Jean Cocteau, *Orphée*, script, 1950.

John loved to work and delighted in the convivial culture of teamwork. He relished communication and every conversation, no matter how temporary or sustained. Once retired, he became an ardent reader of spiritual, metaphysical, and natural-science literature. John had his favorite armchair at Barnes & Noble in Augusta, where he and Elaine visited daily for years. Known for his relentlessly optimistic outlook and idiosyncratic sense of humor, John embodied a love of Maine, a profound respect for nature, and a strong desire for social justice. Both down-to-earth and "in the stars," he remained curious and open-minded his entire life.

A loving husband, father, brother, and son, John is survived by his wife of sixty-three years, Elaine; his son, Brian; his daughter, Julie; his brothers, Richard, Peter, and David; and his sisters, Ruthie, Jane Lindholm, and Sara Fasciano. His parents, Charles and Ruth, brothers William, Charles, Robert, and James, and sister Mary preceded John in death.

From the obituary of John Lee Ault. *Kennebec Journal | Morning Sentinel*, November 4, 2014.

What should stay the same?

A moratorium on gentrification would be good. The thorough gentrification of New York cannot be reversed; the extent of cultural demolition inflicted is disgraceful. We've been brainwashed to think nothing can stay the same, but that isn't really true. The collective and corporate expansionist mind-set that has infected society and so many institutions is profoundly destructive. Downsizing seems to me a more valuable agenda.

From "Questionnaire: Julie Ault." *Frieze* 163 (May 2014): p. 224.

Julie Ault: I consider Spero's engagement with [Antonin] Artaud to be a deep, long, fully felt, inquiring, abundant, empathetic, violent, existential kiss. Her tongue exploring Artaud's disembodied being, at once a philosophical reflection and mirror love. Artaud is a mirror for revealing herself (to herself) and her most extreme reflection and discovery, her placelessness, anguish, and anger. By holding up a mirror image, or a mirror itself that fragments and bounds yet opens onto something unboundable—swallowing up and letting go—Spero conceals and reveals herself. The Codex discloses the intimacy of profound affinity.

The Codex is an arena for Spero's immersion, dueting and dueling with Artaud, which demanded of the artist a new form, a new conception of space—an arena to stage such actions and language, for asserting and inserting her voice. What did it mean for Spero to merge with Artaud, to take him, to plunder his work for her own, while insisting on careful and repetitive attribution, on their separateness? Yet the insistent repetition of the author's name like a mantra at the same time seems to declare her own. Here is Spero.

Christopher Lyon: I love your image of Spero's engagement with Artaud as a violent, existential kiss, with her tongue exploring Artaud's disembodied being. An explicitly sexual mirror image in *Codex Artaud VII*, not reproduced legibly in my book, is essentially an invented hieroglyph (or "spéroglyph," to use Hélène Cixous's delightful coinage) signifying "double," and it appears again in subsequent codices.

This figure reinforces the theme of penetration-as-doubling, and there are several more or less explicit images referring to fellatio. Most obvious is the male figure appearing at the extreme right of *Codex Artaud I*. At his crotch is a female head, tongue extended.

Ultimately, love is redemption, following the Christian paradigm. The dead are rescued from oblivion, given eternal life. By her love, Spero redeems Artaud. In this redeemed state, boundaries are obliterated: male becomes female, and female becomes male. The early incarnation of the Sky Goddess, which later becomes Spero's signature stamped figure (in several versions), is pictured in *Codex Artaud XXV* as combined male and female figures. They are symmetrically bent over, with upper bodies melded, so that they form an inverted U with both male and female characteristics. This odd creature is rendered in a profile "Egyptian" style, the male leg on the left, with a penis at the crotch, and a female leg on the right (seemingly in high heels!), with four pendant breasts hanging from her lower torso.

From "Spero's Subversive Code: An Exchange between Julie Ault and Christopher Lyon." In *Nancy Spero Codex Artaud*. Ed. Julie Ault, pp. 72–74. Venice: Punta della Dogana—Pinault Collection, 2015. Brochure for the exhibition *Slip of the Tongue*.

Wong's harnessing of the similitude of the firefighters' safety net and the Chinese symbol for the celestial is utterly inspired. One of the last paintings he made, *FDNY* is a glorious and emblematic articulation of both Wong's metaphysical core and his exceptional mind; a triumphant meditation on the symbiotic nature of heaven and earth, on the cycle of life and death, and on infinity. In Martin Wong's work, as in his life, the boundaries between dystopia and paradise are abolished, and outward contradictions are unified. Divinity is nested in earthliness.

From "Martin Wong Was Here." In *Martin Wong: Human Instamatic*. Ed. Antonio Sergio Bessa, p. 96. London: Black Dog Publishing; New York: Bronx Museum of the Arts, 2015. Exhibition catalogue.

Helaine Posner and Katy Kline: Occasionally you must find yourselves and the thrust of your work in opposition to each other's ideas, and yet your values remain the same. We would like to know how you navigate through that. Nancy, your feminism must bounce off the fact that Leon is a very powerful . . .

Nancy Spero: Of course, of course. But what irritates me is that women artists are often expected to respond to the idea of the universal—the phallus, the symbol of power and authority. I would prefer to act without constant reference to it, unfettered from rather than in reaction to the male presence. Why should women artists be constrained to respond to male power and control? Let male artists respond to us! Which actually has occurred in various ways since the 1970s. In the *Codex Artaud* I use Antonin Artaud's language to get my frustrations out into the world. The figures—hetero-homo-transsexual—were frequently tiny, my hands could cover them when the kids were going through the studio, but it wasn't just the children. Perhaps I was mocking the giants that had been pouring forth in Leon's *Gigantomachies* and was reacting to the pompous world of post-war American painting, with its huge spaces and gesturings.

HP and KK: The largeness?

NS: The large size of the canvases that male artists do in particular. Not that women haven't done enormous works. I have done fragile linear paper works measuring 20 inches by 100 or 200 feet or more, but to me, in its characteristic manifestations, it is a male, and an American, phenomenon. My figures were small, this was a ploy, just as working on paper was intentionally subversive, a personal rebellion, recognizing that I would no longer do "important" work, in terms of collectors' preferences for canvases of the "proper" dimensions. Nobody was buying my work in any case. This was against the art world, the male establishment, and continues over time—male dominance, male wars, males as perpetrators. I reassessed my work when I began the *War Series*. Coming back from Paris to New York, I was fed up with oil painting night after night. I had to find my own way in the 1960s.

From "A *Bomb* Specific Piece by Julie Ault." *Bomb*, no. 131 (Spring 2015): p. 125. Reprint of a conversation in *Nancy Spero and Leon Golub: War and Memory*. Ed. Katy Kline and Helaine Posner, pp. 20–48. Cambridge, MA: MIT List Visual Arts Center, 1994.

HOW FAR CAN MEMORY AND MEANING BE
STRETCHED BEFORE THE VISUAL BOND SNAPS?

"ONE MAN BEAT HIS WIFE WITH A GOLF CLUB.
WHAT COULD BE MORE MIDDLE CLASS
THAN THAT?"

LIKE ARTAUD'S PEN THAT "SCRATCHED THE
HEART OF LIFE," SPERO'S COLLAGES "SCRATCH"
THE EYE. HIS "GODTHEDOG AND HIS TONGUE."
HER RESPONSE TO CRUELTY CUTTING THROUGH
HOSTILE FLESH. "TO BE SOMEONE/YOU MUST
HAVE A BONE/NOT BE AFRAID TO SHOW THE
BONE/AND TO LOSE THE MEAT BY THE WAYSIDE."
ARTAUD VIOLENTLY REJECTED THE SEXUAL AND
IDENTIFIED IT WITH THE FEARSOME FEMALE
PRINCIPLE THEY SAY, HE WAS REPELLED BY THE
FACT OF BEING BORN FROM HIS MOTHERS WOMB:
"I WAS BORN FROM MY WORKS AND NOT FROM A
MOTHER. . . . THIS IS NO WAY OF BEING BORN TO
BE COPULATED AND MASTURBATED FOR NINE
MONTHS IN A GAPING MEMBRANE WHICH
DEVOURS WITHOUT TEETH AS THE UPANISHADS
SAY." DOES THAT TRIANGLE STAND FOR THE
MOTHER GODDESS?

SHORTHAND. SPERO IS SECRETARY TO THE
APOCALYPSE.

From "1976, 1983, 2015." *Starship*, no. 13 (Summer 2015): p. 98. Reprint of a text by
Lucy R. Lippard. In *Nancy Spero: Torture of Women*. New York: A.I.R. Gallery, 1976.

Julie Ault: We should touch on the conundrum of historical presentation, of making past present (*a new tense?*). Lines of questioning contour the ground. What spirit steers historical inquiry? How is narration or giving account conceived and achieved? How are contexts evoked and freshly created? How do spectatorial, artistic, curatorial, institutional, and presentational roles and aspirations coalesce? How do we do justice to a subject terrain and its complex interacting strata in and for the present?

Looking to another field, natural artifacts embody era. Rock formations, for instance, are capable of revealing the interactions of forces that configured them as well as their own influence on their surround. A rock formation evidences complex events in or across time, but geologists (geological method and sensibility) are responsible for decoding what happened and for telling stories about those events, for constructing histories.

Fareed Armaly: I'm thinking even further afield to eras and rock formations. During the last decade, two concepts emerged regarding the history of now-classic albums. A live format develops, where famous bands re-form for a set of concerts to perform one complete album exactly as it sounded. Meanwhile, a new "making of" TV documentary format analyzes classic albums, returning to the original master tapes, excavating layers of tracks with producers and, if possible, the musicians responsible.

Albums are rarely documents of one live recording event but an artifact created in layers over time in the studio, in a variety of processes where what you stated (. . . capable of revealing the interactions of forces . . .) is applicable. These current options acknowledge both audio- and necrophile. The historical vinyl artifact is now split along being treated as a perfect live re-creation of the album or forensically examining the master recording process. I'd contrast that to the sense of historical vinyl in use by the end of the 1970s, joint expressions of a commemorative listening and the archaeological, forensic search for a sound within, only empowered in a performative bricolage, a historical index erupting (sample, scratch, breaks, and so on) as materialist building blocks for a new contemporary voice.

From "Present Past: A Conversation between Fareed Armaly and Julie Ault." In *to expose, to show, to demonstrate, to inform, to offer*. Ed. Matthias Michalka, pp. 200–1. Vienna: Museum moderner Kunst Stiftung Ludwig Wien, 2015. Exhibition catalogue.

In the morning light, the familiar decaying carpet came into
focus, its surface of biomorphic shapes brought forth by disintegration reminiscent of skin diseases and topographic maps. The
bloodstain wasn't as big as I'd expected—I've seen larger, but
thankfully it had dried and dimmed, blending somewhat with
the faded brown rug. Scraps of this and that spotted the area
and furniture had been shoved to the side along with disorderly
piles of books that must have toppled over.

Emotion at a distance, I inspected the stain and the site—
Dexter style—attempting to objectively reconstruct the incident
from aftermath, hyperconscious of emergent thoughts and of
my own detachment joining with rushes of personal history. I
couldn't decipher how he fell or picture how his body crumbled,
or what hit what on the way down and what exactly had caused
the blood flow; the scene that the initial action produced had
been reconfigured by the emergency team that administered
on-the-spot care, got him out of the living room and into
an ambulance.

From "Ipso facto." In *Afterlife*. Galerie Buchholz, New York, 2015. Exhibition
wall text.

*beech tree 1965   The Letting Go 2006   Aunt Jo's Kitchen 1965
Surtsey 1963   1950 Dance Turned Into A Romance 1980   hair
1979   Hatchet 2013 1970   Soul on Ice 1968   Helms Amendment
1987   Everything was sleeping as if the universe were a mistake
2013   Cab Ride 1995   Fred and Barney and Little Red Riding
Hood 1996   Hall of African Mammals 1962   Unicorns 2011
The Bad Seed 1991   Homestead Act 1938   Indochine 1990
wonderbread 1962   When Earths Grow Thick 1996   Breakfast
Special 2013   Ziggy Stardust 1973   The Sun 1990   purple
unicorn 2016*

From Julie Ault, Roni Horn, and Felix Gonzalez-Torres, *"Untitled" (Portrait of Julie Ault)*. In *Felix Gonzalez-Torres.* Ed. Julie Ault and Roni Horn, n.p. New York: Andrea Rosen Gallery, 2016. Exhibition brochure.

Creating access and affinity was central to Wagner's work. He was committed to the communicative, educative, and transformative power of art and display, and could regularly be found guiding visitors through exhibitions and providing active mediation at every opportunity. His long-term Neue Gesellschaft für bildende Kunst collaborator and friend Leonie Baumann recently said, "He never cares how long the audience has to stand during his speeches that are usually just a little too extensive at exhibition openings, or how many visitors can keep up with him to the end of his exhibition tours that can easily last hours. . . . To understand contemporary art, you need time: end of discussion." (And indeed, when Frank invited Group Material to do a talk in Berlin in 1989, the four of us sat there, incredulous, while he "introduced" us for forty-five minutes, in German, and then suddenly turned to us and said, "OK, now you talk.") A receptive and informed multitude resulted from Wagner's generous narration. [Ingo] Arend reminds us not to "underestimate how strongly those exhibitions helped form a progressive public that is now again under populist attack."

For Wagner, curatorial and creative engagement meant working sensitively and intensively with people, often leading to long-term alliances with artists and colleagues. Many of his relationships were thirty years plus. As in his project concepts, Wagner expressed considerable empathy in his relational conduct. He had true respect for all the occupations and entities that make art and its presentation possible—from artist to audience to institution to funder to critic to docent to gallerist to designer, et cetera—and carefully cultivated professional relationships, no matter how incidental or enduring, holding one and all to his self-imposed standards of rigor, often with transcendent results.

From "Bird of Paradise: Frank Wagner (1958–2016)." *Texte zur Kunst*, no. 104 (December 2016): pp. 230–31.

Duncan MacKenzie: Well, I wanted to take this back to Group Material and go through that nomadic existence, and you existed in this nomadic way for fifteen years. What starts the end of Group Material?

Julie Ault: I understand why you're asking me that, but again, I have to say it's really hard for me to think in those linear terms because it seems like the end is always built into things, or maybe potentially built in. So I can't say the end started at a certain point, after revisiting the paper trail, which jarred memories and discussions. It seemed to me the end was there in the beginning. Yet that's just normal. You know, that's banal almost. I'm not too interested in trying to dramatize a beginning, middle, and end, or the different periods of Group Material. I think you mentioned before we started the formal conversation that there were these different incarnations or iterations of Group Material and Group Material wasn't just one thing. Yes, it was a sequence of configurations and social bodies and so I think there were compositions of the group that were more satisfying to everyone than other compositions. And more effective perhaps. Probably the biggest external factor that fed into the latent ending was the cultural shift that was happening, from the eighties to the nineties or around there, where a lot of the things that I suppose Group Material had been really intent on—our agenda for cultural democracy and the principles that we were interested in activating in a public discourse—were also being taken up, superficially or otherwise—in institutional culture.

Tim and I were talking the other day and talking about the interest in Group Material that is regenerated. I said, well, you know, if the *Show and Tell* book came out now and culture had really changed, if culture and society had changed dramatically between then and now, then the book on Group Material would just be a bit of historical interest. But instead it speaks to the present because even though there have been a lot of changes, there hasn't been any sea change. There hasn't been any massive

shift in the art industry or in the larger social system, etc., so
I think the group's work is still relevant.

From "Episode 322: Julie Ault," interview by Duncan MacKenzie, Abigail
Satinsky, and Bryce Dwyer. *Bad at Sports*. Podcast audio. October 31, 2011.
Reprinted in *Say It While You Still Mean It: Conversations on Art and Practice.*
Ed. Terri Griffith, Duncan MacKenzie, and Richard Holland, pp. 75–77. Chicago:
Open Engagement, 2017.

The good fortune of realizing limitations. The bind of medium specificity. The desire to deepen. The shocking pleasure of jumping into an ice-cold lake.

They took account of the unexpected color combinations they saw on houses in Greece. They slept in a lava field at the base of a massive cinder cone and collected rocks of reddish-brownish black and leaves of silvery gray-green to replicate paint colors for their home in the Mojave.

Dual citizenship. When the pink and the blue meet and merge at dusk in the desert.

Undaunted by massive bodies of information.

Accumulating data over belongings.

Night after night beneath the Milky Way's solar systems, stars, comets, asteroids, dark matter, dust, gas, and massive black-hole center. Sometimes alone: in wonderment, gauging the moon, awaiting UFOs, feeling small, feeling supreme, and sometimes accompanied—identifying constellations or playing a game of perception and scale shift. Predicting which of the soundless planes circumscribing the sky high above will hit which star. "Shoot, that one only missed by a quarter inch."

From "The Conjunction of Martin Beck." In *Martin Beck: rumors and murmurs.* Ed. Matthias Michalka, p. 9. Vienna: Museum moderner Kunst Stiftung Ludwig Wien, 2017. Exhibition catalogue.

Julie Ault: More than one psychoanalyst and theoretician has talked about how photography and photographs can obscure actual memory by creating a stand-in that takes the place of the dynamic aspect of memory, which would imagine something past as more present. Some believe that photographs conceal memory rather than delivering it.

Sadie Benning: I think about that regarding language, too. If I think about gender and all of the possibilities each person could manifest about who they are in terms of gender, not just their biology or what they're assigned, but how they feel inside throughout their life from day to day, moment to moment, I feel like each person has a wide range, maybe some less than others, but I think every individual is very much their own gender. But when it comes to the constrictions of a binary language system, we end up with a limited ability to perceive as a consequence.

JA: Language is expressive, and it's also oppressive. It prevents as much as enables. You're spot on about time, too, because, of course, time telling through clock time, as we know it, is an invention of the Industrial Revolution. Calendars from other epochs and cultures work with natural phenomena. But the Industrial Revolution changed the conception and measure of time in Western culture.

SB: I don't know about you, but I don't have a lot of memories from my childhood of having conversations with adults—I can't remember any of them. [*Laughs*]

JA: Yeah. I can only remember one conversation, where I asked my mother what sex was. I was sitting in the bathtub.

SB: I have two conversations I remember. One with my grand-father when it was New Year's Eve, and he was explaining to me why people were celebrating. I was, like, "What?" He was trying

to explain the clock and the calendar and why we would be celebrating the end of one year. I remember it felt like this very
extreme thing to relate to. I learned a lot about math from my
grandfather, so I loved talking to him about numbers. But just
something about the calendar seemed crazy to me.

From "Julie Ault in Conversation with Sadie Benning." In *Sadie Benning: Shared Eye*. Chicago: The Renaissance Society at the University of Chicago, 2017. Exhibition catalogue.

The global shipping and shipbreaking industries have exploited loopholes in existing regulations to continue "toxic colonialism," to avoid both the high costs and the dangers to native workers and home countries of detoxifying operations. Around 90 percent of the world's retired ships are run ashore on beachfront in Bangladesh, India, Pakistan, China, and Indonesia during high tides. American ships are sought after in South Asia for their high-grade steel. The ships are broken down primarily to recover steel, but practically everything found on a vessel is recyclable in one market or another.

Bangladesh remains one of the biggest importers of end-of-life ships; the scrap industry provides the country, which has no iron ore of its own to speak of, with nearly all of its steel. The industry emerged there in the 1960s after a cyclone left the Greek ship *M D Alpine* wrecked on the then-pristine beach of Sitakunda, Chittagong, where it remained for years. When people informally scrapped the vessel, taking everything to use, recycle, or sell, shipbreaking was born in Bangladesh.

From "Itinerary." In *Stories of Almost Everyone*. Ed. Aram Moshayedi. Los Angeles: Hammer Museum, 2018. Exhibition catalogue.

It's not that I'm mapless or lack agenda, but my search takes an idiosyncratic route in an undefined expanse, informed as much by the desire to articulate what it is about the person–the artist–the writer–the activist David Wojnarowicz that moves me so as it is by whatever tributary, incident, internal byway or distant landscape beckons, by what I don't know that I'm looking for. I want to let go of time, lose myself in discovery, and dive deep. Memory figures in, how could it not: forgetting and remembering our proximity in the downtown matrix of the eighties and early nineties—the years bracketed by the plague. David's voice paves the path, arousing trust and warmth for a man I never met, a man whose soulfulness revolutionizes.

From "Notes toward a Frame of Reference." In *David Wojnarowicz: History Keeps Me Awake at Night*. Ed. David Breslin and David Kiehl, p. 75. New York: Whitney Museum of American Art, 2018. Exhibition catalogue.

Contributors

Julie Ault is an artist, curator, writer, and editor whose work encompasses the fields of exploratory research, exhibition making, and publishing. Across these disciplines, Ault emphasizes relationships between cultural production and politics. Her projects, which frequently adopt curatorial and editorial activity as a creative practice, are characterized by a keen focus on social and collaborative modes of artistic and historical production, often with Ault engaging as a shared author.

Dancing Foxes Press is a Brooklyn-based independent book publishing platform focusing on collaborations with artists, writers, and scholars. Past projects include *Rosa Barba: The Color Out of Space*, *Leidy Churchman: Emergency*, *Before Pictures* by Douglas Crimp, *Les Goddesses / Hemlock Forest* by Moyra Davey, *Zoe Leonard: Available Light*, and *Amy Sillman: the ALL-OVER*, among many others.

Galerie Buchholz is a contemporary art gallery with exhibition spaces in Cologne, Berlin, and New York. The gallery is jointly run by Daniel Buchholz and Christopher Müller. Galerie Buchholz recently collaborated with Julie Ault, Danh Vo, and Heinz Peter Knes on a project about the collection of artist Martin Wong, which included the book *I·M·U·U·R·2*, 2013. In 2015, at Galerie Buchholz in New York, Ault organized *Afterlife*, an expansion of her installation for the 2014 Whitney Biennial, which, in her words, "unites artworks, artifacts, texts, and publications as equivalent participants in a conversation about disappearance and recollection."

Nicolas Linnert is a writer and editor living in New York. He is a regular contributor to *Artforum* and has also written for numerous artist publications, exhibition catalogues, and magazines, including *X-TRA*, *Camera Austria*, *Frieze*, and *Starship*. His editorial practice extends to audiovisual media, and he recently collaborated with the artist Moyra Davey on her film *Wedding Loop*. Previously, he served as editor and programs manager at Artists Space, New York.

Filiep Tacq has worked since 1984 as an independent designer, specializing in books, art catalogues, and artist books. He has taught at the Sint-Lucas Instituut, Ghent; and the Jan van Eyck Academie, Maastricht; and has worked on publications by Francis Alÿs, Ibon Aranberri, Marcel Broodthaers, James Coleman, Moyra Davey, Lili Dujourie, Dominique Gonzalez-Foerster, Abbas Kiarostami, Juan Muñoz, Pedro G. Romero, and Thomas Shütte, among other artists.

Acknowledgments

The idea for this book derived from a writing invitation from Dominic Eichler and his interest in my "chronology of thinking" as expressed over time through written excerpts. Thank you, Dominic! The notion that a portion of a text might embody a core thought was planted in my mind years ago when Cerith Wyn Evans and Galerie Buchholz isolated one such fragment from a piece I wrote and used it as a key element in a catalogue and exhibition of Cerith's work.

I am grateful to Heinz Peter Knes for his stunning cover photograph, which visually bespeaks the structure and atmosphere of the book's interior. Heartfelt thanks to Lucy R. Lippard for her vivid, in-depth, and generous introduction that calls forth overlapping ideals and histories that gave rise to much of this volume. I am indebted to Filiep Tacq for the book's elegant, superb design; to Christopher Müller and Daniel Buchholz for their engaged input and ongoing support; to Karen Kelly and Barbara Schroeder for their deft and gracious shepherding of the publication process; and to Nico Linnert, for coorganizing and coediting this book and for vital and precious dialogue throughout the process.

Behind the scenes, Martin Beck has long been a crucial and sensitive respondent to my unripe drafts and has substantially contributed to my publication work and thinking in general. I am endlessly grateful to past, present, and future collaborators, my friends who continue to inspire, and to the many artists, curators, editors, gallerists, scholars, publishers, cohorts, and colleagues who have asked me to lend my voice and write something with or for them over the years. Thank you.

Published in 2017 by Dancing Foxes Press, Brooklyn,
and Galerie Buchholz, Cologne/Berlin/New York

© 2017 Dancing Foxes Press, Brooklyn, and
Galerie Buchholz, Cologne/Berlin/New York

Texts by Lucy R. Lippard and Julie Ault © the authors

In addition to the correction of typographical errors and inadvertent
grammatical slips, the reprinted texts in this book have been minimally
edited for consistency.

ISBN: 978-0-9986326-4-3

Edited by Julie Ault and Nicolas Linnert
Design by Filiep Tacq
Copyedited by Karen Kelly and Barbara Schroeder
Editorial assistant: Sophia Larigakis
Proofreading: Sam Frank

Printed and bound by Brizzolis, arte en gráficas. Madrid
This book is typeset in Ehrhardt MT and Grotesque MT and printed on
Sirio Sabbia 115 gr and Lessebo Design Natural White 115 gr.

Library of Congress Control Number: 2017950609

Dancing Foxes Press
387A Nostrand Avenue
Brooklyn, NY 11216
www.dfpress.us

Galerie Buchholz
Neven-DuMont-Straße 17, 50667 Cologne
Fasanenstraße 30, 10719 Berlin
17 East 82nd Street, New York, NY 10028
www.galeriebuchholz.de

Distributed by
Distributed Art Publishers
artbook.com

Jacket: photograph by Heinz Peter Knes

Printed in Spain